es

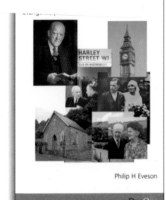

Philip H Eveson

Day One

Series Editor: Brian H Edwards

Day One

TRAVEL
WITH

Martyn **Lloyd-Jones**

❸ Bart's, bombs and brilliance

His training under one of the finest physicians of the day and his experience in treating London's poor and wealthy, all proved to be important preparations for the work that was to make Lloyd-Jones so prominent in the future

St Bartholomew's Hospital, London, commonly referred to as 'Bart's', was one of the leading hospitals of the land. It had an international reputation for medical excellence, giving rise to the popular saying: 'You can always tell a Bart's man, but you can't tell him much.' So many of the medical trainees were from well-to-do backgrounds—educated at some of the renowned public (i.e. private) schools of England, such as Eton and Harrow—and had often completed a medical degree before entering to Bart's. These students could be very self-confident and eager to demonstrate their cleverness but Martyn had no such background and was much more reserved. However, there was no need for this sixteen year old medical student to call attention to his brilliance for it was obvious to all. It came as no surprise when, at the age of twenty-one, Martyn gained the degrees of MRCS (Member of the Royal College of Surgeons), LRCP (Licentiate of the Royal College of Physicians), and MBBS (Bachelor of Medicine and Bachelor of Surgery) with distinction in medicine.

Martyn began his training at Bart's half way through the Great

Facing page: King Henry VIII Gate built in 1702 on the site of the original main entrance to St Bartholomew's Hospital

Above: bomb damage from a Zeppelin

War. Because he was a medical student he was exempt from military service when conscription was introduced in 1916. His brother Harold, who had by this time gone to the University College of Wales, Aberystwyth, to study law, was called up for service and joined the Royal Welsh Fusiliers.

The new inventions that came into being at the turn of the century were put to deadly use during this period. Though the worst of the war was taking place at sea and on mainland Europe, it

❺ Welsh wonder

Lloyd-Jones left medicine to proclaim good news to a depressed area of South Wales. Soon his diary was full of midweek engagements to preach all over Wales

At the beginning of 1927 Martyn experienced three of the most stressful occasions in a person's life: he got married, changed jobs and moved house. The wedding took place on Saturday, 8 January, at Charing Cross Chapel. Among the gifts Martyn and Bethan received was one from the former Prime Minister, Lloyd George, a patient of Tom Phillips. The honeymoon was spent at the Kistor Private Hotel, Torquay in South Devon. This whole week cost just £17, including room service, daily papers and telephone calls! Bethan never forgot the time when she literally sat at Martyn's feet in their hotel room while he went

over the main points of a sermon he was preparing. They moved to Aberavon on Tuesday, 1 February a couple days before the welcome service.

The future home of the new preacher and his wife was to be 57 Victoria Road, a ten-minute walk from the church. As the house was not quite ready for occupation they stayed with one of the church members and their first night together was nearly their last. Having become used to electricity in London, they left the gas light on after it had been turned off at

Facing page: Wedding day, 8 January 1927

Above: Aberavon with Port Talbot steelworks and docks in the distance

Above: Martyn Lloyd-Jones in the 1970s

Thanksgiving Service, Westminster Chapel was filled to capacity when over 3,000 people remembered with affection the life and ministry of this humble man who had touched their lives for the better. His sermons continue to be widely published and have been translated into many languages. They have even attracted scholarly attention resulting in a number of PhD theses. To mark the centenary of his birth, the National Library of Wales mounted an impressive exhibition of books, letters, photographs and videos.

1 Fun, fire and the future

A warning from a teacher and a narrow escape from death led the mischievous, soccer-loving lad who became Britain's greatest 20th century preacher, to think more seriously about his future destiny

The story of Martyn Lloyd-Jones begins in Cardiff, South Wales, at the close of the 19th century, when Queen Victoria was still on the throne and the Boer War had just begun. He was born on 20 December 1899 over the grocery shop that his father owned at 106 Donald Street in the parish of Roath. The register of births records his name as 'David Martyn Jones' and this is how he was officially known until he went to secondary school. In practice, his father had decided that instead of plain 'Jones' the family would be known as Lloyd Jones but it was not until much later that the names were hyphenated. Although in later life everybody knew Lloyd-Jones by his middle name, from his earliest years he was called by his first name, David.

Martyn was the second of three academically bright boys born to Henry and Margaret. His older brother, Harold, born two years earlier, thought of becoming a solicitor and began studying law at Aberystwyth before his untimely death at the age of twenty. The younger brother, Vincent, arrived two years after Martyn. He later entered Jesus College Oxford and became

Above top: Lloyd-Jones was born at 106 Donald St on the corner with Dalcross St, Cardiff. The former corner grocery shop is now a stained glass studio. The Albany Hotel, built in 1895, stands on the opposite corner

Above: A general view of Donald St

Facing page: The monument erected to Daniel Rowland in 1883

President of the Oxford Union. Like his brother Harold, he studied law and was eventually appointed a High Court judge and was knighted for his services. He died in 1986, outliving his brother Martyn by five years.

His father, Henry Lloyd Jones, employed a few assistants to help with the business. In addition, like most middle class families of that period, they had living with them a servant girl, a teenager called Catherine Jenkins. One event that stuck in Martyn's memory from his Cardiff days was the frightening experience of falling down the staircase from top to bottom.

In 1905, the year that Cardiff was given city status, Martyn's father sold the business, left this largely English-speaking, cosmopolitan life and headed back to the Welsh-speaking, sparsely populated countryside, in the heart of south west Wales. The grocery shop had not been a great success and in any case he felt his health would be better served if he returned to where his roots lay. He put in an offer that was accepted for the general store in the little village of Llangeitho.

Henry Lloyd Jones had grown up on his parents' farm in the Rhydlewis district of south Cardiganshire. This area is now part of Ceredigion, named after the Welsh prince Ceredig, and includes the towns of Aberystwyth, Cardigan and Lampeter. Not far away lived Margaret or 'Maggie' as everyone called her, the girl who became Henry's wife. Maggie's family, the Evanses, were also farmers. They lived at the large Llwyncadfor farm, where Maggie's father had become a successful breeder of horses from the Welsh cob to the hackney and shire. Their nearest market town was Newcastle Emlyn which lay on the south side of the river Teifi in the neighbouring county of Carmarthen. Llangeitho was situated further northeast, between Lampeter and Aberystwyth.

The Lloyd Jones family travelled by train from Cardiff to

Top: Lloyd-Jones as an infant

Above: *Harold, Martyn and Vincent (left to right) in 1913, the year of the bicentenary celebrations of Daniel Rowland when Martyn was greatly impressed by the open-air preaching in Llangeitho*

Above: Martyn aged about four (second from the left) with Harold (second from the right) posing for the camera with other children during a dancing class at a small private school in Connaught Road

Carmarthen where they could change for the Aberystwyth connection. This train took them via Lampeter to the little station at Tregaron. These were exciting times for the young boys and Martyn remembers how a pony and trap brought them from the station to their new home in Llangeitho.

Primary school

They had hardly settled before David Martyn with his older brother Harold Lloyd were admitted to the infants' department of Llangeitho primary school on 5 April 1905, although Harold was quickly moved to standard one of the Juniors. The day was not a good one for the harassed headmaster, because three out of his staff of four were absent through illness. He was responsible for about 130 pupils who came from Llangeitho and the surrounding farms and hamlets.

Above: The old 'Albion' stores, now also the Llangeitho village shop and post office

Daniel Rowland of Llangeitho (1713–1790)

Llangeitho has been associated with the name of Daniel Rowland, one of the leaders of the 18th century Methodist Revival in Wales. His preaching attracted thousands from all parts of Wales to this remote spot in the Cardiganshire countryside. George Whitefield, the outstanding evangelical preacher in England and friend of John Wesley, once visited Llangeitho at the time of an open-air communion service and believed he saw 'perhaps ten thousand from different parts'. Rowland was the curate of the church which lay near the river Aeron. When the unsympathetic bishop removed Rowland's licence to preach, the people built a chapel in 1769 on the other side of the river in the parish of Capel Gwynfil. From the chapel house Rowland would enter in his black gown through a little door that led straight into the pulpit. The village where the chapel was built adopted the name of the old Llangeitho ecclesiastical parish. Lloyd-Jones considered Rowland to be the greatest preacher since the apostle Paul. At the time of writing, attempts were being made to establish the Daniel Rowland Heritage Centre in the parish hall next to the Anglican parish church building, where Rowland is buried.

Top: Llangeitho parish church rebuilt in 1819. A stone slab in the church marks the spot where Rowland is buried

Left: The monument erected to Daniel Rowland in 1883

Above: The Calvinistic Methodist chapel rebuilt in 1813. The monument to Daniel Rowland stands close by

The 'British' school, established in 1869 by the Nonconformist 'British and Foreign Schools Society' to provide free elementary education (similar to the 'National' schools which were set up by Anglicans), came under local council control through the Education Act of 1902. The headmaster, Edward Jones, had been at the school since 1882; the four other teachers—three ladies and one man—were all unqualified. When it rained, and it can be drenching rain in these parts, the children, wet through from walking great distances, would be sent to houses nearby to dry out. The school playground often became a lake through poor drainage, and the toilets, described in the head teacher's logbook as the 'offices', were in a deplorable condition. It was not until late October when the temperature was near freezing that the classrooms were heated. This was not always a blessing,

for the coal stove frequently billowed out smoke into the building, making everywhere unpleasant and dirty.

Despite the efforts of the Attendance Officer, school attendance could be very erratic, with the monthly market at Tregaron always affecting numbers. In addition, the many events that helped to keep the community together forced the school to close completely. There were days off not only for the Llangeitho Fair in November and the annual Horse Show in February, but also for special occasions in the life of the churches. These included singing festivals, Sunday School and harvest festivals and special preaching meetings. There were also more unusual occasions, such as an auction sale at one of the farms or the time when the headmaster burnt his foot or had an attack of lumbago. Despite the many difficulties, when His Majesty's Inspectors came to the school in October 1909, they gave it a good report.

Though the school was in the heart of Welsh-speaking Wales, the policy of the British government was that children should be taught through the medium of the English language. Children were even discouraged from speaking their native language in the school playground. Martyn and his brothers, on the other hand, came to Llangeitho as English speakers. Even though their parents spoke Welsh to each other, it had become the practice in many middle class homes to speak in English to their children. Their mother had been brought up by an English step-mother, so it was natural for her to converse in English with her own children. As Martyn got to know the children of the area better he begged them not to speak to him any more in English. He wanted to be thought of as a Welsh lad like his mates.

Life in the village

As a young child, Martyn showed little interest in reading books; his older brother Harold was the studious one. Among Martyn's favourite pastimes was playing football with the local boys or watching the farmers with their dogs bringing the sheep into the pens. In later life he continued to enjoy sheep-dog trials and was fascinated watching the skill of footballers on television.

Mixing with the older boys he had the opportunity of smoking an occasional fag end and longed for the day when he would become a grown-up and be able to smoke freely like a man. Once, when he was entrusted with the keys of the house, he felt so important that he decided to buy himself a packet of Woodbines. His father later found them in his pocket, marched the mortified son to the shop where he had purchased them and made him hand them back to the equally embarrassed shopkeeper. Martyn came to smoke about ten

Above: School register showing the names of Martyn and Harold

Above: Llangeitho school today

cigarettes per day and even to use a pipe, but he gave it up entirely from the age of thirty after he realised he was becoming a slave to the habit.

Compared with many other children in the village, Martyn was well provided for, and when Christmas came round his parents did not encourage him singing carols to earn money. Young Martyn, however, wanted to give it a try and enjoyed the experience of carolling with a small group of boys and girls—and of course, receiving his quota of pennies. However, when he realised that the money the children were collecting was for their mother's funeral he was deeply upset and it left an

In what Class at Admission.	Successive Standards passed in this School (I., II., &c.) I II III IV V VI VII	In what Class at Withdrawal.	Date of Leaving and Return of the "Child's School Book."	Copy of the last Entry made in the "Child's School Book."			Name.	Occupation.
Inf.		Inf.	29 1 06	Left for Hampshire			Thomas Davies	Farmer
Inf.	08 09 10 11		7 3 12	different for work			David Davies	Tailor
Inf.	08 09 10 11		10 10 41	Left for education			Henry Rees	Rly assistant
Inf.	09 10 11 12 13 14	15	23 7 55	admitted Joy			David Evans	Smith
Inf.	05 06 07 08 09		13 9 09	Ysgoroin County			Henry Lloyd Jones	Shopkeeper
Inf.	07 08 09 10 11		20 1 10	Left for County School			Henry Alex Jones	
Inf.			5 12 05	for London			Thomas Roberts	Provision Merchant
VII			06 31 5 06	Service			Evan Williams	Carpenter

Left, top: A grinning Lloyd-Jones aged six on his grandfather's pony at Llwyncadfor

Left, below: Lloyd-Jones in his late sixties on John and Mari Jones' farm at Llanymawddwy, North Wales, still grinning from ear to ear

Facing page: Martyn and his father outside the new shop and home, called the Albion, soon after it was rebuilt

indelible impression on his mind.

Martyn loved to spend his Easter and summer holidays with grandfather Evans and the horses at Llwyncadfor. He enjoyed carrying buckets of water and horsemeal and leading some of the quieter horses to the railway station and helping to put them into horseboxes for their journey to some large show in Carmarthen, the West of England or London. If anyone asked him at that time what he wanted to be when he grew up, the immediate reply would have been, 'a groom'. He never lost his love of horses and commented later: 'For me, there is no animal that beats a horse for grace and pomp.'

Nothing fascinated him more than to listen to adults relate interesting stories of the past. All kinds of people would pop into his father's store for a chat and some came into their home and entertained the family with interesting accounts of bygone days. Later in life, Martyn too was good at making a story live. He did not often relate stories in the pulpit but he could so narrate incidents from the Bible that people would be literally holding on to their seats.

Besides various trips to local agricultural and horse shows, there came a very special outing when Martyn was about eight. He went with his father by train to an agricultural show in London. Instead of returning by train, they

met a local squire who insisted they return with him in his new Alfa Romeo. The motorcar had not long been invented and was a luxury item at the beginning of the 20th century. What a thrill for this impressionable boy!

The three hundred mile journey back to Cardiganshire was an eventful experience. It took two days and nights to return home. They had to contend with an overheated engine and tyre punctures. The squire was forced to purchase four new tyres and inner tubes from a certain Mr Morris in Oxford. Little did they realise at the time that this dealer would become Lord Nuffield, the producer of the Morris Minor car.

Sobering experiences

Martyn's carefree early life came to a sudden and dramatic end when he was ten. In fact, he nearly lost his life altogether. Farmers had come to his father's shop to pay their outstanding bills with gold sovereigns on Wednesday evening, 19 January 1910. They had stood talking and smoking in the clothing section of the store and some tobacco ash had obviously fallen on fabric and lay smouldering; it ignited in the early hours of Thursday morning when everyone was asleep. Martyn was rescued by his father who threw him from an upstairs window into the arms of three men standing below. The whole house and shop went up in flames. Of the few

162

July 26. *Archwilwyd y cofrestrau, a chafwyd hollol gywir.*

J. Rowlands.

July 28th Closed school to-day for the Midsummer Holid It is proposed to re-open September 4th 1911

Sept. 4 1911 School re-opened to-day.
A number of children have left during the holidays. Two - (David Martyn Lloyd Jone Albion Stores - 219 marks and John Davie Pencastell 204 marks. both in Standard have won county Scholarships and intend ente the Tregaron Intermediate School. Sept 25th Edmund Jones Certificated Assistant Tea has been put on the Staff of this school.
The Staff is arranged thus :-
Standards VI. & VII   Edward Jones   (C.
" V   David Davies   (U.
" III & IV   Edmund Jones   (C.
" I & II   Margaret Davies   (U.

Above: Llangeitho school logbook noting Martyn's achievement in winning a county scholarship and the appointment of Edmund Jones as a full-time qualified member of staff. The logbook can be examined in the Ceredigion Record Office in Aberystwyth

Facing page, above: Llwyncadfor farm in its heyday, was a bustling place with many family members, grooms, farm hands and servants

Facing page, below: Llwyncadfor farm lies silent today

items retrieved were the sovereigns now reduced to a solid mass of gold. Martyn moved for a time to his grandparents' home and attended Brongest school.

Life in Llangeitho for Martyn was never the same after this. Although the new building was a vast improvement on the former, he missed the feel of the old home but more importantly, his father never fully recovered from the losses he had suffered. The parents sought to hide their financial difficulties from the children, but Martyn quickly gathered the seriousness of the situation from

unguarded comments made to him by his grandfather Evans.

Martyn also received some stern words from someone who saw his potential. Edmund Jones, a student assistant who later joined the school as a qualified teacher, saw Martyn playing football in the village square and decided to take him aside. He warned him that unless he put his mind to his work he would not gain a scholarship to the County Secondary School like his brother. Knowing that without a scholarship, further education would be out of the question, Martyn took the teacher's warning to heart. He became more serious about his schoolwork and this was rewarded in the scholarship examinations of 1911 when he earned second place, gaining more marks than his brother Harold had done two years earlier.

Something of Martyn's early mental ability had been noted and spread around the neighbourhood in 1909 when the minister of the church asked his Sunday School class: 'Why did Jesus say, "*Lazarus,* come forth"?' After a few moments silence Martyn replied in Welsh: 'In case they all came forth!'

Above: Hills surrounding Llangeitho

When travelling in Wales, road signs will be displayed in both Welsh and English (e.g. Welcome to Wales/Croeso i Gymru). In the more Welsh speaking areas the Welsh text will appear before the English (e.g. Araf/Slow). This applies to Welsh place names also.

Cardiff (Caerdydd)

Cardiff lies at the mouth of the river Taff

Above: Cardiff Castle

on the Bristol Channel. It is easily reached by car from junction 32 of the M4. Parking in the centre at reasonable rates is usually not a problem. InterCity trains link most cities with Cardiff. For local Cardiff buses ☎ 0870 608 2608.

Cardiff became a city in 1905 and the capital of Wales in 1955. Before the First World War, it was the largest coal-exporting port in the world. Today, with the closure of the coalfields, the docks have been dramatically transformed. Both the National Assembly for Wales and the Wales Millennium Centre are situated in Cardiff Bay. Sites of interest in the centre include:

Cardiff Castle, Castle Street, CF10 3RB. ☎ 029 2087 8100 Web www.cardiffcastle.com

The Millennium Stadium, ☎ 0870 013 8600

The National Museum & Gallery, Cathays Park, CF10 3NP ☎ 029 2039 7951. Web www.nmgw.ac.uk Car park at rear (small charge).

The Anglican cathedral lies two miles to the north west of the centre on the banks of the river Taff in Llandaff (bus No.122).

The Museum of Welsh Life (previously known as the Welsh Folk Museum) is in St Fagans about 4 miles from the centre (bus

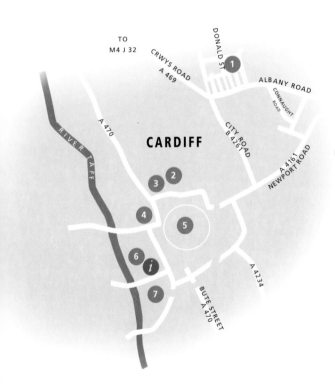

KEY TO PLACES

1 106 DONALD STREET

2 NATIONAL MUSEUM

3 CITY HALL

4 CASTLE

5 SHOPPING CENTRE

6 MILLENNIUM STADIUM

i WOOD STREET VISITOR CENTRE

7 CENTRAL BUS AND RAIL STATIONS

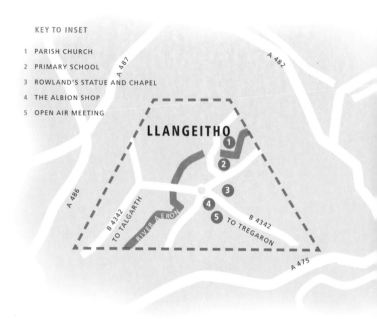

KEY TO INSET

1 PARISH CHURCH
2 PRIMARY SCHOOL
3 ROWLAND'S STATUE AND CHAPEL
4 THE ALBION SHOP
5 OPEN AIR MEETING

No.320). There is ample free parking. ☎ 029 2057 3500. Web www.nmcw.ac.uk/mwl

Entrance to National Museums and Galleries of Wales is free.

Cardiff Visitor Centre, 16 Wood Street, CF10 1ES. ☎ 029 2022 7281.

Llangeitho

A bus service no.516 operates to Tregaron via Llangeitho on weekdays from Aberystwyth bus station. Also nos. 588, 585 from Lampeter. By car take the A487 south from Aberystwyth then left on to the A485 to Tregaron and Lampeter. After leaving Tregaron turn

right on to the B4342 for Llangeitho. From Lampeter follow the A485 toward Tregaron then bear left on to B4578 and at the crossroads bear left onto the B4342 to Llangeitho.

Coffee and meals are served at the Three Horseshoes Inn, Llangeitho, ☎ 01974 821244.

Above: Llangeitho Square

Brongest

This village, the nearest to Llwyncadfor farm, lies between Beulah and Ffostrasol and has no public transport. Nearest bus routes are No. 554 Cardigan to Newcastle Emlyn and No.201 Carmarthen to New Quay. The nearest bus route to the private farm of Llwyncadfor is No. 462 Newastle Emlyn to Llandysul.

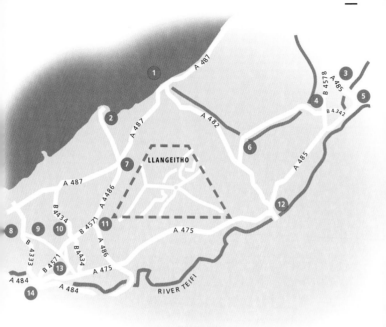

Above: *Early morning mist over the village of Brongest which lies in the Ceri valley. Horses are still bred in the area*

❷ From Wales to Westminster

Lloyd-Jones owed his love of history, particularly the 18th century period, to his own church background and the influence of his history teacher

Martyn moved with his family to Llangeitho at the time of the last Christian revival to sweep Wales. While much of Welsh-speaking Wales was aflame with religious enthusiasm Llangeitho, which had seen even greater spiritual power in the 18th century, remained unaffected and spiritually dead. The minister and head deacon of the village chapel dismissed those taken up with the revival as 'hot-headed and madmen'.

Martyn's father was a Welsh Congregationalist by upbringing and, as with most Welsh nonconformists of those days, a Liberal in politics. He, like so many of his generation, imbibed the 'social gospel' with its emphasis on the need for change through better education and political action. His wife had been christened in the Church of England and remained at heart an Anglican and a Tory. According to custom, however, she followed her husband when it came to church attendance. The only nonconformist chapel in Llangeitho belonged to the Calvinistic Methodists so Henry Lloyd-Jones had no choice but to attach himself to this place of worship.

Every day Martyn passed the chapel and the statue of Daniel

Facing page: View from Llangeitho school of the graveyard, chapel houses and Methodist chapel

Above: Road to the school from the village passing the chapel and statue of Daniel Rowland

Rowland on his way to and from primary school. On Sundays he would be found with his parents and brothers at the morning and evening services and at the afternoon Sunday School. Because everyone in church professed to be Christian, Martyn did not hear any message challenging him to repent of his sin and turn to Jesus Christ for salvation.

At the suggestion of the minister, when Martyn was just fourteen he and his two brothers became members of the church. This meant that they could take Holy Communion. Instead of being asked about their commitment to Christ, they were questioned on the geography of Palestine. Nevertheless, in the chapel services, the Bible was read and the old Calvinistic Methodist hymns were sung. Although these did not mean much to him at the time, they were stored in his mind ready to come alive in his experience at the right moment.

His interest in people and movements of the past began when he moved to secondary school. But it was an event during the summer of 1913 that left a deep impression on the young teenager. The South Wales Association of the Calvinistic Methodists had asked to meet in Llangeitho that year to celebrate the 200th anniversary of the birth of Daniel Rowland. The Chapel was not big enough to hold those expected to attend, so the main meetings were held in a field to the left of the road leading from Tregaron. A pulpit was erected and enough benches to seat a congregation of about five thousand. Some of the big names of the denomination at that time were booked to preach.

Martyn was overawed by the grand and stately appearance of the preachers and stirred emotionally by their eloquent preaching. It awakened within this thirteen year old a dissatisfaction with the

Above: Howell Harris, Daniel Rowland and William Williams

The Welsh Revival of 1904–5

This revival, which drew worldwide publicity, is often associated with Evan Roberts, a twenty-six year old candidate for the Calvinistic Methodist ministry. In 1904 he had a remarkable experience of the Holy Spirit which led him to hold prayer meetings in his home church at Loughor, near Swansea. These meetings drew large crowds so that within weeks the whole county of Glamorgan was affected. The revival was not confined to places visited by Evan Roberts. The very week that Roberts experienced divine power in his home church, there was a separate movement of the Holy Spirit in North Wales, near Wrexham, under the preaching of R.B. Jones, a respected Baptist minister. The intensity of the revival lasted from November 1904 until April 1905, when it was calculated that there had been 100,000 conversions.

Above: The field where the open air meetings were held in the summer of 1913

services at his own chapel and fuelled an interest in the original preachers of Calvinistic Methodism that was to be so influential in his own unique ministry.

Secondary school days

The small market town of Tregaron is some four miles from Llangeitho. Its county school was one of about ninety-five such schools established in Wales under the Welsh Education Act of 1889; an Act that provided bright pupils with an opportunity to gain a school certificate at the age of sixteen—and one that universities recognised. Tregaron County Secondary School came into existence in 1897, meeting first in the Town Hall, but a new building

Calvinistic Methodism

This Christian denomination, mainly Welsh-speaking, arose out of the 18th century evangelical revival in Wales under the leadership of Howell Harris, Daniel Rowland and William Williams—the author of the hymn 'Guide me, O Thou great Jehovah'. The denomination is also known as the Presbyterian Church of Wales. At one time it prided itself on being the largest of the Welsh nonconformist denominations. While the Methodist movement in England came to be associated with John and Charles Wesley and was called Wesleyan Methodism, the same movement in Wales adhered to the teachings of John Calvin, the 16th century Reformer of Geneva. During the 19th century the Calvinistic Methodists of Wales sent missionaries to northeast India where a remarkable work was done in the Lushai and Khasia hills region among headhunting tribes.

Above, inset: Tregaron County School when Lloyd-Jones attended

Above: Tregaron County School today, now comprehensive. The front part has become the local library and more modern classrooms have been built on the opposite side of the road

Facing page: Tregaron square

catering for a hundred boys and girls was formally opened on 26 May 1899 with G. T. Lewis, a Cambridge graduate, as the first headmaster.

There were no school buses in those days and the journey was considered too long for Martyn to walk each day. His brother Harold had already been at the school for two years and was living in lodgings near the school, so it was decided that Martyn would live with his brother in Tregaron during the week.

Unlike Llangeitho, which was protected from the winds by the surrounding hills, Tregaron was more exposed, and the boggy nature of the area made it feel even colder. Martyn hated his time spent in this raw, damp place away from the family home. In the winter months he suffered from chilblains that added to the misery of his homesickness. His longing for home would intensify through seeing his father returning to Llangeitho without him after a busy day at the market. Many years later, when he saw an expression of sadness on the face of a young girl in the same train compartment as himself, on her way back to boarding school, he knew exactly how she felt. He admitted that he had to hide his face in the book he was reading because of the tears of emotion that flowed.

When he was thirteen Martyn persuaded his parents to allow him to cycle to school each day during the summer term. The pain of lodging again at the beginning

of the Christmas term 1913 was eased slightly when his brother Vincent joined him at the county school. All three brothers were now in 'digs' together in the town.

Despite his longings for home, Martyn did well at school and it was becoming clear to everybody that he was an exceptionally bright pupil with a phenomenal memory. Although he was judged incapable of learning the art of woodwork, he was obtaining top prizes in mathematics. At the age of thirteen, Martyn decided that he wanted to become a doctor, much to the delight of his parents.

Both the headmaster of the school and his deputy, S.M. Powell, were not inhibited by the prevailing opinion of the times, and often spoke Welsh in the classroom. Mr Powell taught History and English, and it was in large measure due to this teacher that Martyn's love of history was first kindled. He encouraged his young pupil to look into the history of his local chapel and gave him a book on Howell Harris. Martyn's enthusiasm for cricket also developed under this same teacher's influence. Years later, Martyn was invited back to the school to speak at the Prize Giving and in his address he paid tribute to his history teacher for emphasising the Methodist revival. He also told his audience that there was no real value in education unless it helped build character and he was grateful that the school had done much in encouraging people to think.

In the summer of 1914 Martyn sat the Junior Central Welsh Board examinations (like our modern day GCSEs) at the same time that his older brother Harold sat the Senior Board examinations (like A levels). Between them they obtained twenty-nine certificates and four supplementaries. Martyn gained distinctions in three subjects including mathematics and chemistry.

Bankruptcy!

However, for the Lloyd-Jones household, as with so many across the nation, 1914 was a year they would have wished to forget. But for them, it was not only the year that shattered the optimistic spirit of the age with the commencement of the First World War, it was also the year in which Martyn's father went bankrupt. The full horror of the situation did not sink in until auction day arrived and all that they owned was sold to the highest bidder. This was a far worse experience than the devastating fire of 1910. It brought to light all the hidden fears concerning the family's financial position that Martyn had nursed since that date.

His father's plan was to emigrate. Ever since a Canadian came to the area and distributed leaflets at the school entitled 'Canada the land of opportunity', the thought had been at the back of his mind. Henry Lloyd-Jones now resolved to take action and stay with his wife's brother in Winnipeg to search for work and a place to live. The plan involved leaving his wife and the three boys in rented rooms in Tregaron until Harold and Martyn had finished sitting their important examinations. They would then sail out to join him. Martyn remembered how heart-breaking it was when the morning came for his father to say goodbye.

From the letters that arrived over the next few months, it soon became apparent that their father, now in his fifties, was not going to find the work he was expecting. He therefore made up his mind to look for something in London and boarded a ship that was due back at the end of July.

Wandering through Westminster

With the school examinations over and the change of plans, Martyn's mother decided to stay with two of her boys at her old home at Llwyncadfor. Martyn, however, because of his commercial skills, was commissioned to go to London to help his father look for a suitable business. On Saturday 1 August 1914, he was put on a train for London to stay with another of

Above: The countryside around Tregaron

Above: *Tregaron bog*

his mother's brothers in Bermondsey. His father's boat was due in London's Surrey docks on 3 August. As this was the day that Germany declared war on France and Belgium, it was judged too dangerous to bring a passenger ship through the English Channel, so his father's boat docked at Plymouth. Henry Lloyd-Jones then came by train to London where Martyn and his uncle met him at Paddington station.

It was an interesting and exciting time for Martyn to be staying in the English capital, because on 4 August, Britain declared war on Germany. That morning, he was in Downing street with his father watching the various cabinet ministers come and go at No 10. It became a regular habit for father and son to walk from Bermondsey to Westminster early each morning. They caught glimpses of Prime Minister Asquith and Lord Kitchener, and clapped and

Above: *10 Downing Street, the home of British Prime Ministers*

Left: *Prime Minister Herbert Asquith, who was Prime Minister at the outbreak of the Great War*

cheered with hundreds of others as a regiment of soldiers marched past on their way to France with a band playing, 'It's a long way to Tipperary'.

However, their main purpose in walking the streets of London was to find a new home and business. Instead of going with his father, Martyn would sometimes help his uncle deliver milk to local homes; this involved measuring out the correct amount from the milk churn into the jugs that people brought to the door. As it happened, his father decided to buy a dairy business, a very popular occupation among the Welsh of London, especially those from Cardiganshire. The owner expected trade to collapse with so many men offering themselves for the war effort and, wanting a quick sale, the price was set at a modest figure. Henry Lloyd-Jones purchased the dairy and the home above the shop with the help of money borrowed from a sympathetic groom at Llwyncadfor. So it was that in October 1914, the Lloyd-Jones family were reunited in their new home at 7 Regency Street, Westminster.

Milk, politics and school

Martyn did not go back to school immediately. The school-leaving age was not raised to fourteen until the end of the Great War, so

Above: 7 Regency Street and the milk barrows

Right: Regency Street today. Apart from the café on the corner with Page Street, the old shops and houses have been demolished

Above, left: *Charing Cross Road Chapel, London, where Martyn attended church with his parents*

Above, right: *Early sea plane on the Thames near Westminster Bridge*

that most children his age would already have found themselves a job. His older brother Harold became an articled clerk in a solicitor's office and Martyn felt he should give up the idea of becoming a doctor and instead help the family finances by training to be a bank clerk. In the first few months at the Regency dairy, however, Martyn's experience on his uncle's milk round meant that he was the one often called upon by his father to help when any milkman failed to turn up for work. It involved him rising at 5.30 in the morning and pushing a three-wheeler barrow with a large churn of milk to the homes around Westminster.

He delivered milk to the Wellington barracks in Petty France, a walk that took him past Westminster Chapel. Little did he think that he would later occupy its pulpit for thirty years. His parents had been encouraged to attend the Chapel by some of the customers who were members of this English Congregational Church, but the family continued their associations with the Welsh Calvinistic Methodists by joining one of the best-known chapels of the denomination in Charing Cross Road.

Above: *wartime Prime Minister, Lloyd George*

Left: *The former St Marylebone Grammar School now used for offices*

Contrary to the previous owner's gloomy expectations, under Lloyd-Jones the business began to flourish so that all debts were eventually repaid. With this upturn in fortune, Martyn and his young brother Vincent were sent to St Marylebone Grammar School in January 1915 to complete their studies.

With the war still raging, the Lloyd-Jones family took an even greater interest in politics. Policy disagreements among the Liberals resulted in Lloyd George becoming Prime Minister. Martyn's father and brothers supported Asquith the outgoing leader, while Martyn supported Lloyd George. Living within walking distance of the Houses of Parliament enabled Martyn to visit the Strangers' Gallery of the Commons on his way home from school. During those war years he heard some stirring speeches from eminent men including his hero, Lloyd George.

Spending so much time listening to political speeches might have affected the studies of many a young person, but not Martyn. In the London University Senior School examinations, which he sat in the summer of 1916, he passed all seven subjects and gained distinctions in five. He applied to the Medical School of St Bartholomew's Hospital, London and, after a preliminary examination and interview, was accepted at the unusually young age of sixteen.

TREGARON BOG
(CORS CARON)

TO DEVIL'S
BRIDGE AND
STRATA
FLORIDA
ABBEY

A 485

B 4343

RIVER TEIFI

TREGARON

P

1

i

2   3

KEY TO PLACES

1   BWLCHGWYNT CHAPEL

2   OLD COUNTY SCHOOL & PUBLIC LIBRARY

3   KITE CENTRE

i TOURIST INFORMATION

TRAVEL INFORMATION

Tregaron

A bus service operates on weekdays from Aberystwyth No. 516 and Lampeter No. 585/588. By car take the A487 south from Aberystwyth then left on to the A485 Lampeter road. The car park is free and toilets are close by.

Over 75% of the population of this market town speak Welsh. International pony trotting races are held twice a year. Cors Caron (Tregaron Bog) is a nature reserve and home to the red kite, an endangered bird of prey. The public library occupies part of the old county

Above: Tregaron square with the bronze statue of Henry Richard 'the Apostle of Peace' (1812–1888) erected in 1893. Born in Tregaron he became a Congregational minister in London, then secretary of the Peace Society and MP for Merthyr Tydfil. The Henry Richard Memorial Library was opened in Smith Square, Westminster, by Lloyd George in 1927

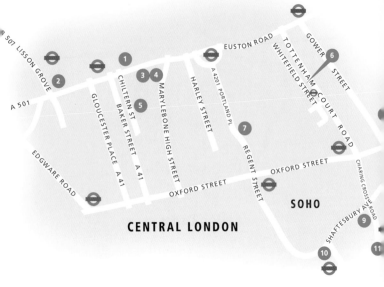

secondary school. Along Dewi Road (B4343) just beyond the Garden of Remembrance, the old National School (Church of England) houses the Kite Centre.

The ruins of the 12th century Strata Florida Abbey are at nearby Pontrhydfendigaid.

Tourist information centre, Dewi Road, Tregaron, Ceredigion, SY25 6JN ☎ 01974 298144.

Refreshments are available at The Cambrian Coffee Shoppe Monday to Saturday.

London Whitefield's Chapel

The original Tottenham Court Road Chapel, known as 'the Dissenters' Cathedral', was built in 1756 and was the largest nonconformist church building in the world. John Wesley preached Whitefield's funeral sermon here in 1770. The old building collapsed in 1889 and a new one was erected in 1899, but with Whitefield's old pulpit still in use. This was the chapel

Borough of St. Pancras
WHITFIELD STREET W1

where Lloyd-Jones was ordained in 1927 (see chapter 5). It was destroyed by a V2 rocket bomb in 1944. The 'Whitefield Memorial Church' was erected on the site in 1957 and is home to 'The American Church in London'. The nearest tube is Goodge Street (Northern line). Buses 10,24,29,73,134 travelling north stop nearby. Because of the one-way system, the same buses travelling south use Gower Street.

Left: *A monument to Charles, the brother of John Wesley, and writer of many famous hymns. It can be found behind Holy Trinity Marylebone Road in Marylebone High Street in a Garden of Rest where once stood the old St Marylebone Parish Church demolished in 1949. The body of Charles, his wife and son Samuel are buried in the old graveyard*

Charing Cross Chapel

It lies near the junction with Shaftesbury Avenue. The nearest underground is Leicester Square (Northern, Piccadilly). Buses 14, 19, 24, 29, 176 stop nearby.

The earliest Calvinistic Methodist congregation in London was founded at Cock Lane in Smithfield in 1774. They eventually moved to Jewin Crescent in 1823. From the mother church other congregations were established. One met in Grafton Street in 1849 which moved first to Nassai Street and then in 1885 to Charing Cross Road. There were 600 members in 1900 which increased to 1,222 by 1937. Lloyd-Jones' minister was Peter Hughes Griffiths (1871–1937). The end of the 19th century until the outbreak of the Second World War saw a period of unprecedented growth in the membership of the London Welsh chapels. Much of this was due to the many migrants from Wales who came to the capital during the economic depression that followed the Great War. By 1925 there were in London thirty-two Welsh language churches belonging to the various Christian denominations.

St Marylebone Grammar School

On the corner of Lisson Grove and Marylebone Road stand offices that incorporate the old school with its hexagonal library and towers. The Victorian

Gothic red brick building was erected in 1857 to house the Philological School, founded in 1792, which aimed to educate the sons of poor clergy and naval and military personnel. In 1908 it was taken over by the London County Council to become the St Marylebone Grammar School. It closed in 1981. The nearest underground stations are Marylebone (Bakerloo line) or Edgware Road (Bakerloo, Circle, District Hammersmith & City). Buses 18, 27 stop nearby.

12 Vincent Square, Westminster

This is where Mrs Lloyd-Jones senior with her two sons, Martyn and Vincent, moved after the death of her husband in 1922 (see chapter 4).

Nearest underground is Victoria (Circle, District, Victoria lines). Buses 2, 36, 185 stop nearby on Vauxhall Bridge Road.

7 Regency Street, Westminster

The block of old houses where the dairy was situated has been demolished and new buildings erected. The nearest underground stations are St James's Park (Circle, District) or Victoria (Circle, District, Victoria lines). Bus 507 stops nearby.

3 Bart's, bombs and brilliance

His training under one of the finest physicians of the day and his experience in treating London's poor and wealthy, all proved to be important preparations for the work that was to make Lloyd-Jones so prominent in the future

St Bartholomew's Hospital, London, commonly referred to as 'Bart's', was one of the leading hospitals of the land. It had an international reputation for medical excellence, giving rise to the popular saying: 'You can always tell a Bart's man, but you can't tell him much.' So many of the medical trainees were from well-to-do backgrounds—educated at some of the renowned public (i.e. private) schools of England, such as Eton and Harrow—and had often completed a medical degree before moving to Bart's. These students could be very self-confident and eager to demonstrate their cleverness but Martyn had no such background and was much more reserved. However, there was no need for this sixteen year old medical student to call attention to his brilliance for it was obvious to all. It came as no surprise when, at the age of twenty-one, Martyn gained the degrees of MRCS (Member of the Royal College of Surgeons), LRCP (Licentiate of the Royal College of Physicians), and MBBS (Bachelor of Medicine and Bachelor of Surgery) with distinction in medicine.

Martyn began his training at Bart's half way through the Great

Facing page: King Henry VIII Gate built in 1702 on the site of the original main entrance to St Bartholomew's Hospital

Above: Bomb damage from a Zeppelin

War. Because he was a medical student he was exempt from military service when conscription was introduced in 1916. His brother Harold, who had by this time gone to the University College of Wales, Aberystwyth, to study law, was called up for service and joined the Royal Welsh Fusiliers.

The new inventions that came into being at the turn of the century were put to deadly use during this period. Though the worst of the war was taking place at sea and on mainland Europe, it

Above: The Square when Lloyd-Jones was a student at Bart's in 1916

St. Bartholomew's Hospital

This is the oldest of the London hospitals, founded in 1123. The poor sick people of Smithfield were cared for by the brothers and sisters of the Priory that was established there at the same time. When Henry VIII closed the Priory, Bart's became one of the four Royal Hospitals administered by the City of London. Among the many notable people who have worked at Bart's was William Harvey, who discovered the circulation of the blood. Attached to the hospital is a medical school founded by John Abernethy in 1822. A decade later it was reputed to be the largest in London. Bart's merged with the Royal London and London Chest Hospitals in 1994 to form the Royal Hospitals NHS Trust.

was brought to the doorsteps of many in Britain when the first German air-raids took place. Instead of sheltering somewhere safe, Martyn, along with everybody else, used to run out into the street to see the awesome cigar-shaped Zeppelin airships in the sky with searchlights playing on them. When a bomb fell near Bart's Hospital, Martyn was quickly on the scene to give a helping hand.

Of the sixty million young men of Europe drafted in to fight, over ten million never returned. Harold, Martyn's brother, was invalided out of the army due to a heart condition. Before the Great War was over, however, another scourge hit the planet. This was the Spanish influenza outbreak when over twenty million people died worldwide. In June 1918, Martyn awoke one Sunday morning to find that he had caught it. His brother went down

Above: *The Square today at St Bartholomew's Hospital*

with it a couple of days later, and although Martyn overcame the infection, his brother, already weakened through his experiences as a soldier, never recovered. He was twenty years old. His body was taken to the parish graveyard near the family home at Llwyncadfor, and buried alongside that of his grandfather Evans who had died the previous year.

The signing of the Armistice took place on 11 November 1918, and like thousands of others Martyn left his work and headed in the direction of Westminster. He saw the members of Parliament file across the road for a short service of thanksgiving at St Margaret's Church, with Lloyd George and Asquith leading the way. Then, in December, he stood for hours to catch a glimpse of the American President, Woodrow Wilson, passing in open carriage with King George V. Lloyd-Jones

admitted later in life that he always was 'a bit of a hero worshipper'.

One of the most distinguished teachers at Bart's Hospital was the King's physician, Sir Thomas Horder. Martyn's outstanding ability at diagnosing patients' illnesses caught his attention as early as 1920. In one case, his diagnosis had been based on his claim to feel an enlarged spleen in the patient's abdomen which Horder's own examination had not picked up. Horder was so impressed that he chose him to be his junior house physician before the actual results of his qualifying examinations were announced. Martyn continued to impress Sir Thomas who soon gave him the position of Chief Clinical Assistant at the hospital.

There were still times in his early years as a student when an emergency at his father's dairy meant that he would be called to

Thomas Jeeves Horder (1871–1955)

Thomas Horder was known as 'the little genius' for the speed with which he was able to arrive at a correct diagnosis. He came to public attention while in his thirties, when he was called to the sick room of King Edward VII. The King's full ashtray was enough to convince Horder that his majesty's chest condition was due to nicotine poisoning. Thereafter the rich and the famous came to his rooms in Harley Street. He was the Physician to Bart's Hospital in the 1920s. In May 1923 he was summoned to Paris to examine the British Prime Minister, Andrew Bonar Law, and diagnosed cancer of the throat with six months to live. Law resigned his public office and died six months later as predicted. Other royal patients included George V, George VI, and Elizabeth II.

Horder had a cool head but a warm heart. He once said to Lloyd-Jones: 'I should be ready to treat Beelzebub himself if he came to my consulting room.' His parents were Congregationalists and in his early student days in London he sat under the gripping ministry of the Reverend Joseph Parker at the City Temple Church, Holborn. Horder later abandoned his early Christian background and accepted a humanistic philosophy. But religion remained a lifelong interest and he always recognised its value for his patients. He was one of the founding members of the Cremation Society. Knighted in 1918, he was created the First Baron Horder of Ashford in 1933. At his memorial service one of his patients, Sir Malcolm Sargent, read the closing words of Bunyan's *The Pilgrim's Progress*.

Above: Thomas Horder (centre) with Lloyd-Jones seated next to him on the right in 1923

do a milk round before rushing to the hospital. On one occasion his early morning work caused Martyn embarrassment and greatly amused his fellow students: while in attendance at one of Horder's out-patients' clinics Martyn felt so sleepy that he only vaguely heard a question put to him by Horder so that he was uncharacteristically hesitant in his reply.

In addition to ward rounds and clinics, there were the more menial tasks such as gathering relevant material for important lectures that his Chief was to deliver. One of the most significant jobs Martyn was given to do in his spare time involved going through the case notes of each of Horder's patients in order to prepare an index of all the diseases he had treated. It was an eye-opener to

Above: Anthony Bowlby's firm in 1919 with Lloyd-Jones standing second from the left

see the kind of conditions suffered by some of the dignitaries of the land, including members of the royal family and cabinet ministers.

For relaxation Martyn learned to play tennis and enjoyed lunch hour musical recitals at St Sepulchre's Church. In the evenings he would occasionally visit the theatre or, even better, the opera house. He also continued the practice he had begun while attending St Marylebone school, of slipping into the Strangers' Gallery of the House of Commons where he heard some of the important parliamentary speeches of the War.

The promising physician

When Martyn was twenty-three he earned the highly respected London University MD (Doctor of Medicine) research degree, again at an unusually young age. He held the Baillie Research Scholarship for eighteen months, investigating a type of Hodgkin's disease called Pell-Epstein disease. Knowledge of this subject was to prove very useful some years later in South Wales and helped him gain acceptance by the local doctors. When he was twenty-four, through Horder's influence, Martyn became the first to benefit from the newly founded St John Harmsworth Memorial Research Fund to study a heart condition known as infective endocarditis. Some of the initial experiments are recorded in notebooks now held in the National Library of Wales. The results were published in 1936 under the title, 'An Experimental Study of Malignant Endocarditis' and appears as an appendix to a book by D.B. Perry *Bacterial Endocarditis*. By February 1925 Martyn had reached the top of his profession, obtaining the letters MRCP

(Member of the Royal College of Physicians).

His reputation in the medical world at the remarkably young age of twenty-five was considerable. If he had continued in this sphere of work there is no doubt that Lloyd-Jones would have become a significant name in medical history. Martyn was given one of Sir Thomas Horder's rooms in 141 Harley Street to set up his own private practice in addition to that of his Chief's.

An older contemporary of Martyn's at Bart's was the eminent physician, Sir Arnold Stott, a heart specialist at Westminster Hospital. He also had a private practice at 58 Harley Street where he lived with

Harley Street, London

Harley Street has been the medical heart of London since the 1830s. It takes its name from Edward Harley, 2nd Earl of Oxford, who married the daughter of the Duke of Newcastle in 1713. The marriage dowry consisted of a large part of the Cavendish Estate in Marylebone known as Marylebone Fields. Earl Harley soon began building on the land and it was planned that Harley Street should provide residences for the nobility and gentry. The Liberal Prime Minister, William Gladstone, took up residence here in 1876. By the beginning of the 20th century it was almost exclusively the place where the well-known physicians and surgeons of London had their consulting rooms.

Horder had rooms at No 141 from May 1901 and after his marriage in September 1902 bought the whole house. The children's nursery was on the top floor and the kitchen in the basement. The ground floor housed the dining-cum-waiting room, a room for the secretary and at the end of the long corridor the consulting room. Part of the basement was turned into a laboratory and dispensary after his wife banned his pathology from the bedroom! First floor rooms were rented out as consulting rooms. It was here that Lloyd-Jones had his own private practice. In 1946 Horder sold the property and moved to Devonshire Place.

Above: *141 Harley Street where Lloyd-Jones held a private medical practice from 1925*

Top: Close-up of 141 Harley Street

Above: St Bartholomew's the Less is Bart's parish church which stands on the site of the ancient Chapel of the Holy Cross. The church tower is the only medieval building remaining at Bart's

his family from 1921; that was the year their son, John, was born, who was to have close associations with Lloyd-Jones later in life (see chapter 7).

Only the wealthy could afford the services of Harley Street doctors. The patients belonging to the King's physician were among the cream of society. They included three Prime Ministers, many leading intellectuals, musicians and poets such as Vaughan Williams, Malcolm Sargent and Rudyard Kipling and the novelist, H. G. Wells. Sir Thomas drew Martyn into this world of high society, frequently inviting him to his country estate at Ashford Chace, Petersfield in Hampshire to enjoy stimulating conversation with the influential personalities of the day. On other occasions, he was taken by Horder to medical dinners where the top people in the profession were present. Martyn was often sickened by the undercurrents of jealousy and criticism that he heard.

Martyn described Horder as 'the most acute thinker that I ever knew.' He respected Horder for his amazing ability to ask the right questions and then use his quick mind to eliminate in a moment all possible explanations for an illness until he arrived at a correct diagnosis. When asked to give a list of the best books to read in medicine, Horder invariably headed the list with W.S. Jevons' work, *The Principles of Science: a Treatise on Logic and Scientific Method*. His high regard for Lloyd-Jones was evident when he passed on to him his personal copy

Top: The entrance to the Smithfield Market

Above: Part of St Bartholomew's Hospital erected in 1842 and enlarged in 1861 showing the memorial to the Protestant martyrs

of Jevons that had greatly influenced his own thinking.

One of Martyn's close friends who became a leading surgeon at Bart's was Geoffrey L. Keynes, brother of the economist, John M. Keynes. Writing of Lloyd-Jones in 1980, Sir Geoffrey remarked, 'I was very friendly with Martyn Lloyd-Jones when we were both working as Chief Assistants at St Bartholomew's Hospital in the early 1920s, he on the medical side, I on the surgical. I greatly admired his intellectual approach to medicine as a profession. I was not the only one of his friends to have these feelings and to appreciate also his humanity as a doctor.'

Besides Horder, Martyn had the privilege of knowing and working with some of the other important names at Bart's. These included Sir Bernard Spilsbury, the Chief Pathologist to the Home Office who was eager for Martyn to work in his own private medical practice. Another consultant physician with whom he was friendly was Geoffrey Evans, the Assistant Professor of Medicine at Bart's Medical School. One autumn day in 1926 he crossed the Square at Bart's to speak to Martyn. He wanted him to know that his part-time teaching post at the hospital was becoming vacant and that Lloyd-Jones' name was at the top of the list for the position. By this time, however, Martyn had other ideas that were to lead him in an entirely different direction.

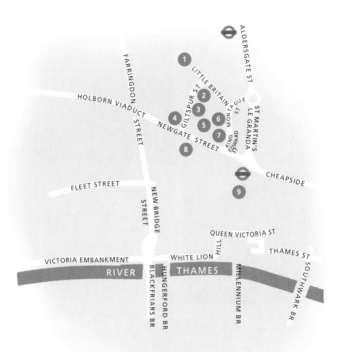

KEY TO MAP

1 SMITHFIELD MARKETS

2 MARTYRS' MEMORIAL

3 ST BARTHOLOMEW THE LESS

4 ST SEPULCHRE'S

5 BART'S HOSPITAL

6 ROWLAND HILL STATUE

7 CHRIST CHURCH STEEPLE

8 THE OLD BAILEY

9 ST PAUL'S CATHEDRAL

TRAVEL INFORMATION

St Bartholomew's Hospital

St Bartholomew's Hospital, West Smithfield, London, EC1A 7BE

Archives & Museum ☎ 020 7601 8152

The hospital is near Smithfield Market and about five minutes walk from St Paul's underground station (Central line). Buses

8,25,56,242,521 stop nearby. The hospital museum is located in the historic North wing. Opening times: Tues. to Fri. 1000–1600 hrs. Closed for public holidays.

Admission free. Historic Bart's & Smithfield Guided Tours start at the Main Gate of the hospital every Fri. 1400 hrs.

Smithfield Martyrs Memorial

Set in the hospital wall near to King Henry VIII Gate is the memorial to the 200 Protestant martyrs who were burned to death near this spot during the reign of Queen Mary.

Above: Memorial to the Protestant martyrs at St Bartholomew's Hospital

Left: St Sepulchre's

Above: A notice at the entrance to St Sepulchre's drawing attention to famous names associated with the church. This was the church where Lloyd-Jones came to listen to lunch hour organ recitals

Church of the Holy Sepulchre without Newgate

Often referred to as St Sepulchre, this is the church where John Rogers was the rector from 1550. Rogers had been the chaplain at the English House in Antwerp and was converted through the preaching of William Tyndale there. He later edited Tyndale's translation under the pseudonym 'Thomas Matthew', and it was Matthew's Bible that was licensed by Henry VIII in 1537. Rogers was the first of the Protestant martyrs to be burned alive at Smithfield under Queen Mary on 4 February 1555. He left a wife and eleven children.

Sir William Wallace Memorial

Near the Martyrs' Memorial is a plaque to the memory of a Scottish patriot who fought for his country's independence. He was captured and brought to London and put to death near this spot in 1305.

Above: 'The Golden Boy of Pie Corner' in memory of the Great Fire of London 1666 which was stopped at this point. The memorial was originally built into the wall of a public house called 'The Fortune of War' which occupied the site before being pulled down in 1910

Christ Church

Edward VI founded in 1552 Christ's Hospital, a foundling school for deserted infants. When it was moved to Horsham in 1902, the General Post Office building was erected on the site, Edward VII laying the foundation stone. A statue of Rowland Hill, the originator of the penny postage stamp, stands on the pavement nearby.

The General Post Office and Museum

Christ Church, Newgate Street

This was one of Christopher Wren's most expensive church buildings erected on the site of the Franciscan Grey Friars church destroyed in the great fire of 1666. Only the steeple remains after it was bombed in 1940. The ruined walls and burial ground are now laid out as a garden. From the Friary buildings

Above: *Rowland Hill the founder of postage stamps*

HARLEY STREET W1
CITY OF WESTMINSTER

Harley Street

Nearest underground is Regent's Park (Bakerloo). Bus numbers 18, 27, 30 along Marylebone Road and 88 in Portland Place.

Little Britain

See *Travel with John Bunyan* p. 112 in this series.

Left: *The Central Criminal Court situated across Newgate Street in Old Bailey where many infamous cases have been tried*

④ Dramatic decisions

Even as a child, Martyn Lloyd-Jones had a deep sense of a power controlling all that happens—not in the sense of 'karma' or 'fate' but of a personal supernatural power shaping the course of events. A gradual but profound spiritual transformation took place in his life that lead to a complete change of direction

Martyn had always been a very religious person and everyone accepted he was a Christian. When the family moved to London their membership was transferred to Charing Cross Chapel, where many of the well-to-do London Welsh worshipped. Martyn particularly enjoyed attending the all ages Sunday School, a common feature of Welsh chapel life. Convinced by the age of seventeen of the Bible's teaching that God pre-planned all that happens, he had great debates in his class and felt very pleased with himself if he managed to win the argument. When he was only eighteen Martyn was appointed overseer of the whole Sunday School for one year.

While he continued to attend church regularly as a medical student, Martyn was not always found in his own Welsh chapel. He was drawn to visit Westminster Chapel to hear the ministry of Dr Campbell Morgan until Morgan left for America in 1917. Martyn had first gone there as a fifteen year old schoolboy to hear Dr Thomas Charles Williams, one of the preachers who had stirred him in the special open-air meetings in Llangeitho.

Facing page: The new Hungerford pedestrian bridge and Charing Cross railway station from the London Eye

Above: The text over the door of the pathology department at Bart's reads: 'Whatsoever thy hand findeth to do, do it with thy might'

Conversion

In 1923 Dr John Hutton, a Scotsman, was appointed minister at Westminster Chapel. Martyn was so gripped by his preaching that he began attending the morning services whenever he could. For the first time in his life Martyn was made aware of the power of God to change lives and sensed a spiritual reality he did not find in his own chapel.

Martyn's medical training at Bart's brought him into contact with people from both ends of the social scale. The condition of London's poor was an eye-opener as he found himself faced with the worst effects of drunkenness and sexual immorality. He also treated those who had everything that money and social standing could offer and he discovered that many of them were equally restless and their lives spoilt by drink and sex. The case histories of seventy per cent of those who came to Thomas Horder's private practice revealed they had nothing more physically wrong with them than that they ate or drank too much.

Martyn began to see that the problem with human beings was neither medical nor intellectual, but moral and spiritual. At the same time he was beginning to sense his own spiritual need: 'My trouble was not only that I did things that were wrong, but that I myself was wrong at the very centre of my being.' The environment in which Martyn worked dismissed the relevance of Christianity for the 20th century. None of the medical consultants known to Martyn were Christians. His own chief believed that scientific knowledge had made the Bible and Christianity redundant. The kind of Christianity that did exist at the hospital in the form of the Student Christian Movement had conceded so much to scientific humanism that Martyn found attendance at their meetings a waste of time.

This brilliant twenty-four year old was clearly exercised about the futility of the human quest for knowledge and pleasure. There had to be more to living than dress, sport, degrees and politics. His twenty year old brother had died when Martyn was eighteen and his father died when he was twenty-two. Both these losses were a severe blow to him. He also saw that the church was failing in its task. Generally speaking, the preachers of the day had no clear

THIS STONE
WHICH STANDS ON THE SITE OF THE HOUSE OF
DAME JOANNA ASTLEY, NURSE OF KING HENRY VI
WAS LAID BY
THE LADY LUDLOW
WIFE OF
THE RIGHT HONOURABLE LORD LUDLOW
TREASURER OF St BARTHOLOMEWS HOSPITAL
AS THE FOUNDATION OF A BUILDING
DEVOTED TO
THE ELUCIDATION OF PROBLEMS
IN THE
NATURE AND TREATMENT OF THE DISEASES
OF THOSE
WHO HAVE SOUGHT RELIEF FROM SUFFERING
IN THIS HOSPITAL
DECEMBER 5TH 1907
DOVE BROTHERS, BUILDERS.   EDWARD B. I'ANSON ARCHITECT

Above: *The plaque to commemorate the opening of the pathology building at Bart's in 1907*

Above: Pontypridd Baptist Tabernacle now a museum

message for the people. The first decades of the 20th century saw amazing advances in communication, but while others gathered round their wireless sets to hear the crackled sounds of the Voice of America, Martyn was concerned that he and others should listen to the voice of God.

By the time he had reached the age of twenty-five, Martyn had already become a true Christian. He later described his experience in these terms: 'For many years I thought I was a Christian when in fact I was not. It was only later that I came to see that I had never been a Christian and became one … What I needed was preaching that would convict me of sin … But I never heard that. The preaching we had was always based on the assumption that we were all Christians.' The change did not take place overnight. In the words of a poem that Martyn was to quote many times, written by Francis Thompson, 'the Hound of Heaven' was after him and, like the apostle Paul, the God who humbled him to confess Christ also called him to a special work.

Called to preach

Nearly every Welsh chapel at that time had introduced into its weekly schedule a literary and debating society; it was considered to be one of the means of attracting and holding the young people. Martyn had first been asked to speak at his chapel's society in 1921 when his subject was 'Modern Education'. The next occasion was in March 1924. Under the title of 'The Signs of the Times' he made a scathing attack on all the present crazes to which people gave so much attention. Even though the young people

Above: Pontypridd Baptist Tabernacle pulpit from which Lloyd-Jones gave his first talk in Wales

disagreed with him violently, he was a 'hit' and they invited him to speak again the following year.

In the basement room of Charing Cross Chapel on Friday 6 February 1925 he told his audience of how he had felt compelled to speak on 'The Tragedy of Modern Wales'. It was a devastating criticism of the attitudes of the Welsh and concluded with a rousing call to return to the strengths of the 18th century Methodist Fathers. Loud and long applause followed as the speaker sat down.

A reporter from the *South Wales News* was present and Martyn found that he had made the headlines the following morning: 'Modern Wales, A Sweeping Indictment, London Welsh Lecture'. In typical journalistic style the reporter had gone for the hard-hitting criticisms that the speaker had made but had failed to relate the positive message of his address. A full-length editorial column followed in the next issue attacking the speaker and the speech. The minister of Charing Cross Chapel wrote a letter to the editor in support of Martyn but the criticisms rumbled on for some time and the young London Welsh medic had suddenly become something of a celebrity in the land of his birth.

The address clearly indicated the revolutionary change that had taken place in Martyn's life. But that same address caused a number of his hearers to wonder whether the proper place for this twenty-five year old doctor should be in a pulpit rather than in a surgery. Earlier in his life he had a premonition that he might one day be a preacher but now the call to the Christian ministry became very strong. In a letter to his best friend from the chapel, who had gone to Aberystwyth to prepare for the Calvinistic Methodist ministry, Martyn unburdened his heart. He had felt the criticisms made in the Welsh press very keenly, especially the suggestion that he was all talk and no action. What the critics did not know, as he revealed to his friend, was that before delivering the address, he had made up his mind that after his final MRCP examinations in 1925, he would change course and practise what he was preaching.

Martyn preached for the first time at a mission hall for down-and-out Welsh people in the East

Left: Lloyd-Jones in his early thirties—Cardiff 1932

End of London. Preaching invitations arrived from Wales but these he declined. He did agree, however, to address the East Glamorgan annual conference of the Union of Welsh Societies at Pontypridd in April 1925. His lecture was similar to the one he gave at the Charing Cross Chapel. Again, he met with strong opposition although there were few who did not recognise the power and freshness of the message.

Many doubts had crept into Martyn's mind since he had first decided to leave medicine for the ministry. His minister was far from happy at him considering such a move. Some thought he should combine medical practice with the ministry of preaching, but he had too high a view of the Christian ministry to think of becoming a part-time preacher. Until those doubts were resolved he felt he should not take any more preaching engagements.

From the Spring of 1925 until the Summer of 1926 Martyn was in great turmoil of spirit. He lost over twenty pounds in weight. The call to preach would not leave him. More and more he was led to see the futility of earthly ambition and applause, and that his future lay in proclaiming the good news of Jesus Christ. Both at home and in his research room at Bart's, he had some remarkable experiences of the love of God. By June 1926 the struggle was over; his mind was made up, he would be a preacher of the gospel.

Capturing his bride

June 1926 was also the time when another significant decision was announced: Martyn proposed to Bethan Phillips, the girl of his dreams, and was accepted. He had seen Bethan occasionally as a boy and admired her from a distance when he visited Newcastle Emlyn market with his grandfather.

Bethan was the daughter of Dr Tom Phillips, Martyn's Sunday School teacher at Charing Cross and a well-respected Harley Street eye specialist. The Phillips' family came from Newcastle Emlyn, and Bethan and her brothers would often spend their holidays there. Her grandfather, Evan Phillips, was the minister of Bethel Calvinistic Methodist Chapel in the town. He had not only experienced the power of the 1904 Welsh revival but the previous nationwide revival of 1859. When revival broke out in Newcastle Emlyn in 1904, Tom Phillips sent Bethan aged six and her eight-year-old brother, to stay with their grandparents. Their mother was naturally concerned about their schooling but their father argued

Top: Bethan Phillips aged about eighteen, in Welsh costume

Above: Newcastle Emlyn market today

Above: Evan Phillips (1829–1912) the minister of the Calvinistic Methodist chapel in Newcastle Emlyn for fifty-two years

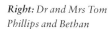

Right: *Dr and Mrs Tom Phillips and Bethan*

that they had the rest of their lives to get an education, but they might never witness another revival.

When the Lloyd-Jones family first filed into the chapel after moving to London, Bethan remembers how they occupied the pew immediately in front of her own family. It was her older brother Ieuan (pronounced 'Yaiyan') who had become Martyn's best friend. In the same year that Martyn entered medical school, Bethan, who was eighteen months older, commenced her own medical training at University College, London. She had stunning good looks and with parents who dined with people in the public eye, Bethan was not short of suitors. With so many proposals of marriage, Martyn did not stand a chance! To make matters worse his conservative

approach to dress, and his decided lack of enthusiasm for most sport did not go down too well with the ladies. In Martyn's address to the debating society in 1924 he spoke of those who thought too much of their physical bodies to the detriment of their souls and he made a negative reference to the habit of bathing daily. Bethan was not present on the occasion but it must have been an embarrassment to learn that her father, in supporting the serious note in Martyn's address, had made a comment that brought the house down. He said, 'Our Bethan is for ever in the bath'!

Persistence and patience paid off, and after several early attempts had failed, romance blossomed from Easter 1926. In a letter to Ieuan at the time of their engagement he wrote, 'I know that I am beyond a doubt the

Left: The Calvinistic Methodist Theological College Aberystwyth, opposite the pier and next to the old Aberystwyth university buildings

Facing page: The statue of Thomas Charles Edwards, a convert in the 1859 revival while preparing for the Calvinistic Methodist ministry and the first principal of the university. It was erected in the grounds of the university facing the sea

luckiest man on the face of the earth'. He also added, 'I want to preach more than ever and am determined to preach. The precise nature of my future activities remains to be settled, but nothing can or will prevent my going about to tell people of "the good news."'

Coming to Wales

Martyn's decision to be a preacher and to get married was momentous enough but another crucially important matter concerned where they would live and where he would preach. As he talked this through with his minister, some matters at least were clear to him. In March of the

The Forward Movement

This is the popular name for the home mission work belonging to the Calvinistic Methodists. It was officially known as 'The Church Extension and Mission Work'. It began through the evangelistic work of the Rev. John Pugh in 1872. Seth Joshua and his brother Frank joined the work and became the 'leading lights'. The aim was to reach working class people with the gospel in the industrial areas of Wales. They had great success and large Forward Movement halls were built to accommodate the people. Seth Joshua died just two years before Lloyd-Jones came to Sandfields.

the denomination's home-mission work, popularly known as the 'Forward Movement'. A meeting was arranged for Martyn to discuss openings with the Superintendent, the Rev. Richard Rees, who found himself in a most unusual situation. The idea of a Harley Street doctor enquiring about ministering in the poor, grimy, industrial areas of Wales was unheard of. Not only that, but when he showed some surprise and tried to dismiss Martyn's desire he was respectfully challenged, 'Really, Mr Rees, why should you be surprised? Don't you believe what you preach?' The meeting ended with the realisation that Martyn would need to follow the denominational procedures for entering the Christian ministry before any further decisions could be made.

After his local church and the London Presbytery had given their formal approval an opening came for him to preach for the first time in Wales at Beechwood Park, Newport on 11 November 1926. This more prosperous area of Newport at the time was not what Martyn had in mind. However, another invitation came from a Forward Movement Hall (known as 'Sandfields') in Aberavon, Port Talbot, asking him to preach at the end of November. He was immediately drawn to the place and the people. Martyn returned with his fiancée to preach again on 12 December. This was, in fact, the first time Bethan had heard him preach. He was officially given a call to become the pastor and he replied positively just prior to Christmas 1926.

previous year he had visited the denomination's theological college at Aberystwyth where Ieuan was studying. As a prospective student Martyn had an interview with the principal but soon decided that the way forward for him was not via the college and into some well-established pulpit. He had a strong desire to work as an evangelist among the poorer, working-class people of Wales. His background had given him some insight into the conditions of those without work or who were sick and receiving no money. Before he died his own father had urged him not to forget the poor. These were times before the social benefits available today.

The one possible opening was

Right: John Pugh who began the Welsh 'Forward Movement'

Facing page: Beechwood Park Chapel. It was a branch from Havelock Street Presbyterian Church of Wales. The Building was erected at a cost of £8,000 and opened in December 1923

The press got to hear of Martyn's decision to become a preacher in South Wales before any formal announcements had been made. A local Port Talbot reporter had managed to draw out from the church secretary the truth of what was happening and sold his story to the London newspapers. It was a great embarrassment to Martyn on Tuesday, 14 December to find national newspapers carrying such headlines as 'Harley-Street Doctor to become a Minister'. For two or three days reporters were outside 12 Vincent Square, where he now lived with his mother and brother. He resolutely refused to give any interviews or to pose for any photographs.

Martyn was particularly upset because he had not given a hint of his intentions to the medical chiefs at Bart's, not even to Horder. They all heard of it first through the press reports. Sir Bernard Spilsbury was 'exceedingly sorry'

and Horder was understandably hurt that Martyn had not discussed the matter with him. Thankfully, the strain in relationships was only temporary, and his friendship with Horder remained unbroken.

Despite all the excitement and fast moving action, Martyn continued working at Bart's until the end of the year, writing up the results of his experiments. Sir Thomas Dunhill, the well-respected surgeon at Bart's, wrote to him: 'I was indeed surprised but … I admire very much a man who plans his own life and goes ahead with it regardless of the multitude who would like to arrange his life for him.' After breaking the news about the brilliant young physician under the heading 'From palpitations to pulpitations' the weekly magazine *John Bull* commented, 'Hats off to Dr Lloyd-Jones'.

Pontypridd

By road from Cardiff on the A470 and by train from Cardiff General.

Pontypridd Museum, Bridge Street, Pontypridd CF37 4PE. ☎ 01443 490748. Free admission. Open Monday-Saturday 1000–1700hrs. This former chapel where Lloyd-Jones gave his first address in Wales was originally built in 1861 and rebuilt 1910. It closed in 1983 to become first a cultural centre and in 1991 a museum. They have kept many of the fittings including the gallery, pulpit and organ.

Further along the A470 toward Merthyr Tydfil turn off onto the B4285 for Aberfan (see chapter 7).

Above: The view from the Pontypridd to Porth railway

Left: 12 Vincent Square where the family moved after his father's death

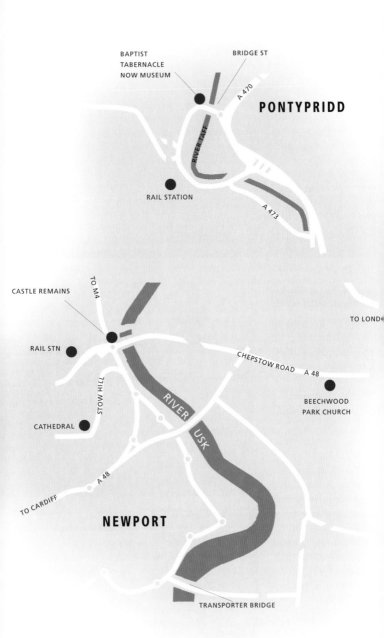

BAPTIST
TABERNACLE
NOW MUSEUM

BRIDGE ST

A 470

PONTYPRIDD

RIVER TAFF

RAIL STATION

A 473

CASTLE REMAINS

TO M4

TO LONDON

RAIL STN

CHEPSTOW ROAD   A 48

STOW HILL

RIVER USK

BEECHWOOD
PARK CHURCH

CATHEDRAL

A 48

TO CARDIFF

NEWPORT

TRANSPORTER BRIDGE

Above: The Newport Transporter Bridge

Top: St Woolos Cathedral

Above: Tredegar House

Newport City

Newport can be reached by car on the M4 motorway and by rail on the Paddington to Swansea line. It received city status in 2002. St Woolos Anglican cathedral is at the top of Stow Hill and a 14th century ruined castle lies beside the river Usk near the centre. Tredegar House, a 17th century mansion, is to the west of the town. Admission to the Park, Gardens and Visitor Centre is free and open all the year but entrance to the House is seasonal and there is a charge. ☎ 01633 815880.

The most significant landmark is the largest remaining example of a Transporter Bridge left in the world. It was opened in 1906 and stands 75 metres above the river Usk. It provides a crossing at all stages of the tide which in 6 hours can rise more than 45 ft (15.2 m). It carries passengers free and cars at 50 pence each. It operates summer and winter. For further details ring ☎ 01633 250322. Website:

Newport Tourist Information Centre, John Frost Square Newport NP20 1PA

Caerleon Tourist Information Centre, ☎ 01633 422656.

⑤ Welsh wonder

Lloyd-Jones left medicine to proclaim good news to a depressed area of South Wales. Soon his diary was full of midweek engagements to preach all over Wales

At the beginning of 1927 Martyn experienced three of the most stressful occasions in a person's life: he got married, changed jobs and moved house. The wedding took place on Saturday, 8 January, at Charing Cross Chapel. Among the gifts Martyn and Bethan received was one from the former Prime Minister, Lloyd George, a patient of Tom Phillips. The honeymoon was spent at the Kistor Private Hotel, Torquay in South Devon. The whole week cost just £17, including room service, daily papers and telephone calls! Bethan never forgot the time when she literally sat at Martyn's feet in their hotel room while he went over the main points of a sermon he was preparing. They moved to Aberavon on Tuesday, 1 February a couple days before the welcome service.

The future home of the new preacher and his wife was to be 57 Victoria Road, a ten-minute walk from the church. As the house was not quite ready for occupation they stayed with one of the church members and their first night together was nearly their last. Having become used to electricity in London, they left the gas light on after it had been turned off at

Facing page: Wedding day, 8 January 1927

Above: *Aberavon with Port Talbot steelworks and docks in the distance*

Top: Bethlehem, Sandfields, as in Lloyd-Jones' time
Above: Sandfields today

the mains by their host. When the supply was turned on again early next morning, lethal town gas soon filled the bedroom where they were sleeping. It was the quick thinking of Bethan that saved the day. Waking up with a thick head and hearing the hissing gas, she jumped out of bed and opened the windows.

The new appointment

Port Talbot had never seen so many reporters since the town first came to public attention in January 1924 when the Member of Parliament for the area, Ramsay MacDonald, became Britain's first-ever Labour Prime Minister. This time the place was buzzing with interest at the thought of a twenty-seven year old Harley Street physician coming as a missioner to Aberavon. The Forward Movement Hall was packed for the welcome meetings on Thursday, 3 February 1927.

It could not be a normal induction service of a minister to a

---

Sandfields, Aberavon

Sandfields is what the congregation called their place of worship and should not be confused with the modern large housing estate nearer the shore. The name chiselled out in the stone arch above the entrance is 'Bethlehem F M Hall'. 'F M' stands for Forward Movement, which explains why the local people described it as 'The Forward'. The church began through Calvinistic Methodist outreach to the navvies (labourers) who worked on the new docks. What became known as the Lesser Hall facing Pendarvis Terrace was built in 1897. A larger building was erected alongside it in 1914 to seat 500 people. In 1933 'the Annex' was added to accommodate the growing Sunday School and as an 'overflow' area for the congregation. Lloyd-Jones was the eighth pastor of the church. Ministers since Lloyd-Jones have included John Thomas, Gwynn Williams and Peter Jeffery.

Above: Victoria Road, Sandfields, today with No. 57 one of the terraced houses on the left of the picture and on the immediate right No. 28 where the Lloyd-Jones family moved in 1932

new pastorate, because Martyn was not an ordained minister. It was only later that a request was made for Lloyd-Jones to be ordained. At the South Wales Association meetings at the end of August, Martyn appeared for questioning along with other men who had come through the regular channels, including his own brother-in-law, Ieuan Phillips. Lloyd-Jones spoke with such conviction and earnestness that the decorum of the occasion was broken with shouts of praise and sobs of emotion. The unusual nature of Martyn's case was heightened by the fact that he was given the honour of preaching at one of the sessions and of addressing the young people. It was unheard of for a ministerial candidate to play such a prominent part.

His ordination finally took place during the first ever Association in London and again he was asked to address the young people. Because no Welsh chapel was large enough to accommodate everyone, they secured the loan of Whitefield's Tabernacle. George Whitefield, the outstanding 18th century Methodist preacher, was one of Martyn's heroes. The date, 26 October 1927, would never be forgotten in the Lloyd-Jones household. On that day when he was ordained, his wife gave birth by Caesarian-section to their first child, Elizabeth. The following morning some of the Welsh newspapers reported the news of 'the Ordination Baby'.

Preaching at Sandfields

Many in Wales wondered why Martyn was turning his back on fame and fortune to become a preacher. Local medical practitioners seriously believed that his real intentions were to set himself up in general practice or as a consultant. Martyn was much amused when he overheard two women on the bus talking about the Harley Street specialist who had come to 'the Forward' as a missioner. One said to the other: 'Oh, yes, I've heard that the doctors are doing very badly in Harley Street just now, so no doubt he was glad to get away and take up this work'! Enthusiastic Labour Party workers, realising that his family had Liberal connections, were convinced he had come to stand for Parliament as a Liberal candidate. Some in the denomination were jealous of him and unhappy that he was allowed to bypass the normal channels for entrance into the Christian ministry. One Swansea minister commented: 'He may be a doctor of medicine, but he is not a doctor of divinity! What does he know about theology?'

Martyn could not have come to South Wales at a worse time. The optimism that existed immediately after the Great War was short-lived. By 1921 severe unemployment was affecting Wales more acutely than other parts of Britain. Following the Wall Street stock market crash in 1929, the Great Depression brought further misery. No area was more deprived than Port Talbot. The dole queues were long, and many of the school children had insufficient food and clothing. Around the Sandfields' Hall about five thousand people lived in overcrowded slum conditions. Though the Christians were appreciated for their care, the inhabitants were generally indifferent about religion. Barely ten per cent of them attended a place of worship. The previous pastor had left in 1926 'with a broken heart' being so

Above: The first church building at Sandfields was erected in 1897 and later called 'the Lesser Hall'

Above: Looking toward the mountains with the houses of Aberavon barely visible from the sea shore. Bethan Lloyd-Jones was fearful that the sea would eventually engulf the area. One night when she was alone in the house with baby Elizabeth with a gale force wind blowing at high tide, she prayed fervently that the Lord would take away her fears and give her peace. The result was complete deliverance from her phobia

discouraged with the small congregation and a large debt to pay off on the building.

E.T. Rees, the newly appointed church secretary of Sandfields, had been brought up to go to church, but he knew nothing of the reality of the Christian message. The gospel he preached was one of social action. Lloyd-Jones won the confidence of this man from the start and he was one of the first of a steady stream of converts. Foul-mouthed, heavy drinkers of Irish, English as well as Welsh backgrounds were subdued under Martyn's preaching. One changed life was Mark McCann, a former miner in his early sixties, who sported a waxed moustache of incredible length. He could not read or write but spent his time picking fights at fairgrounds. Under the influence of drink he was unbeatable and to make matters worse he had an uncontrollable temper. He was brought to Sandfields one Sunday evening and through the preaching of Lloyd-Jones his life was remarkably changed. Bethan Lloyd-Jones later taught him to read.

Bethan herself became a convert at this time and confessed, 'I was for two years under Martyn's ministry before I really understood what the gospel was … I thought you had to be a drunkard or prostitute to be converted.' Martyn's messages showed her that with all her religious background she was a sinner in need of forgiveness like those who had no religion. A Spiritist medium who lived nearby was attracted to attend by seeing the numbers who passed her house on their way to the Hall. She was converted and testified of how on her first visit she sensed the presence of a clean power.

Many of the previous attempts to attract people to the church, such as the musical evenings and the dramatic society, were discarded by Lloyd-Jones. But he encouraged the Monday evening prayer meeting, and within a couple of years it became the best-attended mid-week event, with between two and three hundred people present. Lloyd-Jones would ask one of the men to begin with a prayer, Bible reading and a hymn, and then the meeting was left 'open' for individuals to pray. There were many moving occasions especially when converts prayed for the first time or when someone's prayer seemed to bring everyone into the felt presence of God. One early convert, Harry Woods, was disappointed not to be going straight to heaven from such a meeting instead of going home. Appropriately, this same man died suddenly a few years later after leading the Monday prayer meeting in a most heavenly way.

Lloyd-Jones adapted the Wednesday Fellowship hour so that it became a time of open discussion on practical areas of Christian living. As for the

Above: Bethan Lloyd-Jones' Bible class that first met at the manse and moved to the church as numbers grew

Above: *The Brotherhood with Lloyd-Jones (circled) taken in the early 1930s*

Saturday evening Brotherhood, instead of it being like a social club, he stretched the minds of the men, using the open discussion method to deal with biblical and theological issues. A deep spiritual bond soon developed and in the summer of 1927 Lloyd-Jones took them to Llangeitho, to develop their interest in Daniel Rowland and the 18th century revival. It was the first of many such annual day-outings to places of historical interest.

When Lloyd-Jones began his ministry, the membership of the church stood at 146. Some of these people only became true believers in the years that followed. In his first year at Sandfields he dropped the candidates' class, the one fruitful way many churches at that time were able to add names to the membership roll especially from among the young people. He considered it a dangerous practice to associate church membership with teenage years. Only those who gave credible evidence of Christian profession were allowed to remain on the church roll and in 1930, for instance, 17 people were removed because they 'proved themselves unworthy of membership'. Over the same period 77 were added to the church 'from the world'. During the eleven years that Lloyd-Jones ministered at Sandfields, over 500 people were converted and joined the church. When he left, the membership stood at 514.

Wider work

In his first year at Port Talbot, Lloyd-Jones had mid-week engagements at fifty-four places in South Wales. Soon he was preaching all over the Principality, in village chapels, large town churches and in the open air on isolated farms in the Welsh mountains. He preached at Water Street Presbyterian Church,

Below: A report in the Wrexham Advertizer of Lloyd-Jones' visit to the Forward Movement Victoria Hall in Wrexham in October 1935. It was common for his name to be misspelt

Carmarthen, for the first time in 1928. The presbytery felt it needed a special service to emphasise the centralities of the Christian Faith after one of its ministers, Tom Nefyn, a popular Welsh preacher, was censured and later suspended from office for denying the basic Christian truths. Thereafter, they continued to hold a special service on the last Thursday of September with the same preacher. For fifty-one years Lloyd-Jones kept this appointment.

Lloyd-Jones preached in North Wales as frequently as once a month, including Anglesey, Holywell and Wrexham. The size of the meetings was continually commented on in the Press and it was clear that no one else could consistently gather such numbers. Occasionally, some of the Labour leaders, like Aneurin Bevan, the prominent Labour Member of Parliament for Ebbw Vale and Minister of Health in 1945, could command a crowd, but not midweek and in all parts of Wales. Such was his influence at this time that one academic has argued that Lloyd-Jones and Aneurin Bevan were the two foremost men in keeping South Wales from communism in the 1930s.

Welsh people, as Lloyd-Jones was well aware, could easily be moved emotionally. This was why, unlike some Welsh preachers and Pentecostal evangelists of his day, his sermons aimed first to inform the mind. However, they were never dry and academic but warm and passionate. It was, as he once described preaching, 'logic on fire'. In his evangelistic messages there were no long drawn out appeals. He certainly urged people to submit to God in Christ, but he never encroached on what he felt to be the work of the Holy Spirit to move people to respond. Often it was only later he heard of people converted through his preaching.

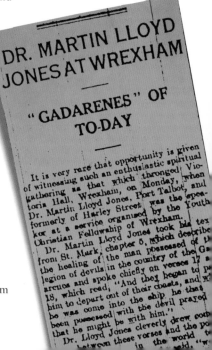

DR. MARTIN LLOYD JONES AT WREXHAM

—

"GADARENES" OF TO-DAY

—

It is very rare that opportunity is given of witnessing such an enthusiastic spiritual gathering as that which thronged Victoria Hall, Wrexham, on Monday, when Dr. Martin Lloyd Jones, Port Talbot, and formerly of Harley Street, was the speaker at a service organised by the Youth Christian Fellowship of Wrexham.

Dr. Martin Lloyd Jones took his text from St. Mark, chapter 5, which describe the healing of the man possessed of a legion of devils in the country of the Gadarenes and spoke chiefly on verses 17 and 18, which read, "And they began to pray him to depart out of their coasts, and he that had been possessed with the devil prayed that he might be with him."

Dr. Lloyd Jones cleverly drew comparison between these verses and the people in the world to-...

Above: The annual Whit Monday Sunday School parade around the streets of Aberavon in the early 1930s with Lloyd-Jones and the men of the church leading the way

Physician of souls

As a pastor he was greatly appreciated for his care and wisdom. One English newspaper reported, 'He has spent, they say, a small fortune in giving practical help to people in need of money, has helped them to clear off arrears of rent and even to buy their homes.' Others were given free medical advice. An embarrassing problem for the Lloyd-Joneses when they came to leave was a cupboard full of bottles of alcoholic liquor that men converted from a life of drunkenness had left with them.

The *News Chronicle* produced an article on Lloyd-Jones entitled, 'A Physician of Souls'. It reported how he shook the locality out of its despair with a fresh display of spiritual power and went on to show that 'it was no passing wonder', for years later 'the congregations still overflow the church... No whist drives, bazaars or worldly side-shows, no dramas except the great drama of salvation ... The "physician of souls", who shuns publicity, draws thousands to hear his message in all parts of the Principality. He will not stand for a Press photographer. But his name is a household word in Wales.'

During the summer of 1932 a Welsh minister in Canada invited him to preach in Toronto for nine Sundays. While he was there, Lloyd-Jones was asked to take a series of meetings at the Chautauqua conference near Buffalo in the United States. Other speakers that week included Mrs Franklin Roosevelt and the well-known agnostic, Julian Huxley of London. Although Lloyd-Jones was a complete unknown, by the time of his final meeting, the venue was switched to the large auditorium where 6,000 people

Above: Statue of Aneurin Bevan in Queen Street Cardiff

Below: Lloyd-Jones with E.T. Rees, the church secretary on a 'brotherhood' day out. In a letter to him, Lloyd-Jones confessed, 'You were undoubtedly the most vital factor in my ever going to Sandfields'

listened in awe to preaching they had never experienced before. He made a second visit to North America in 1937 preaching in a number of Presbyterian churches in Pittsburgh, Philadelphia and New York.

Despite his busy life, Lloyd-Jones always made time for his family and never forgot them when he was away. After his return from his second trip to America, there were presents for all: two dresses for Bethan which she judged were 'perfect in every way', a doll for Elizabeth and a brown teddy for their new arrival, Ann, born in the Spring of 1937. When on holiday, he would take with him some weighty theological book to read in the mornings but then spend the rest of the day playing with the children and sightseeing.

The end of the beginning

In the autumn of 1937, Lloyd-Jones was assured that his time at Sandfields was drawing to a conclusion. After eleven-and-a-half full and happy years in South Wales he was beginning to feel the strain. On a couple of occasions he could not complete his sermon due to voice failure. This was found later to be due to wrong voice production.

A call came in January 1938 to become the minister of an influential Presbyterian congregation in Marylebone, London. A little later, there was a move to secure his services as an evangelist to Britain. His own denomination was anxious to keep him in Wales and sent a deputation of six men to urge him

Above: Martyn and Bethan with Elizabeth and Ann in the Summer 1938

to stay. They indicated the possibility of his succeeding to the position of Principal at the denomination's college at Bala, North Wales, where his gifts could be put to full use in preparing final year ministerial students.

He turned down the call to Marylebone much to the relief of his own people. But their joy was short-lived. At a special Church Meeting held after the communion service on Sunday 8 May, 1938 the Church minutes records, 'To the profound regret and sorrow of the Church the Pastor announced his resignation on the grounds of ill health.'

Though he knew it was right, it was still hard to leave the people they had grown to love. He ensured that the church was not left leaderless, presiding over the meeting on 23 June 1938 which resolved to extend a call to his successor, the Rev. W.M. Jones of Pontrhydyfen, near Port Talbot.

The very weekend that Martyn

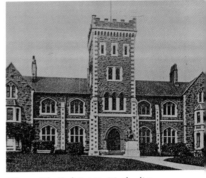

Above: The Calvinistic Methodist Theological College, Bala

announced his decision to resign, he received a letter from Dr Campbell Morgan, the minister at Westminster Chapel, London, suggesting the possibility of sharing the preaching there for six months. At the end of July 1938 the Lloyd-Jones family left their Victoria Road home and went to live with his mother at 12 Vincent Square, not far from Westminster Chapel.

KEY

1 SHOPS

2 SANDFIELDS CHURCH

3 BUS STATION

4 LEISURE CENTRE

5 NO. 57 VICTORIA ROAD

6 NO. 28 VICTORIA ROAD

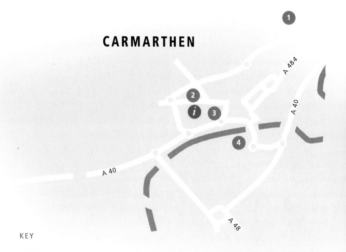

KEY

1 ROMAN AMPHITHEATRE

2 WATER STREET

i INFORMATION CENTRE

3 BUS STATION

4 RAILWAY STATION

Left: *Port Talbot, 1930.*

TRAVEL INFORMATION

Port Talbot

This industrial port lies at the mouth of the river Afan in Swansea Bay and has recently become the County Borough of Neath and Port Talbot. The port was named after the local squire, Christopher Rice Mansel Talbot, for cooperating with English industrialists in constructing the docks that were opened in 1837. A new tidal harbour was opened in 1970. It is one of Europe's leading steel producers.

The old borough of Aberavon (an English corruption of the Welsh *Aberafan* meaning 'the mouth of the Afan') is preserved in the name of the Parliamentary constituency.

A bracken-covered mountain overlooks the town, while hidden by the blast furnaces lies a splendid three-mile stretch of sand known as Margam Sands. Across the harbour and river, the sand continues toward Swansea for a further two miles.

From a wilderness of sand-dunes, sometimes as much as sixty feet high, a beach has been created.

Nearby is Margam Country Park with the ruins of Margam Abbey and a museum of early Christian memorial stones. Four miles up the Afan valley lies the Afan Argoed Country Park with nature trails and a Welsh Miners' Museum of Coal.

The London Paddington to Swansea railway and the M4 motorway pass through the town centre. National Coach operators run from London Victoria Coach station. Local buses stop by Sandfields church.

Tourist Information Centre: Pontneddfechan, Nr Glynneath, SA11 5NR, ☎ 01639 721795

Carmarthen

It can be reached by rail on the Swansea to Fishguard line, by bus No. 701 from Cardiff and Swansea and by car along the M4 and A48.

The town is the administrative centre of South West Wales. Places to visit are the castle remains dating back to Henry I, the Roman Amphitheatre and the Carmarthen Heritage Centre.

Tourist Information Centre, Lammas Street, Carmarthen, ☎ 01267 231557

Above: *Plaque on the side of Water Street Welsh Presbyterian Chapel in memory of Peter Williams (1723–96) another leader in the 18th century Methodist revival in Wales. He was later accused of heresy. His edition of the Welsh Bible with notes was very popular*

6 War and Peace

For the second time Lloyd-Jones moved from Wales to Westminster on the eve of a world war. He saw a regular congregation of 2,000 dwindle to 150. After the war, numbers grew rapidly until nearly 2,000 people attended both the morning and evening services

Lloyd-Jones' ministry as assistant to Campbell Morgan began in September 1938 when over 2,000 gathered to hear him. At this stage, although Campbell Morgan had other thoughts, Lloyd-Jones considered the Westminster Chapel appointment as a temporary arrangement. He was expecting to hear from Wales, but a controversy arose over his nomination for the principalship of the Bala Theological College. Lloyd-Jones regarded this as providential and it led to Campbell Morgan announcing to the congregation on Sunday, 23 April 1939, 'He has now accepted our invitation, and becomes not assistant, but associate-pastor.' The Christian press was agreed that his coming to London would be for the benefit of the church universal.

Martyn accepted the call to be co-pastor with Dr Campbell Morgan only a few months before the outbreak of the Second World War. It was an uncertain time for everyone. Martyn was not sure whether he would be called up for medical service, and when that proved negative, both he and Campbell Morgan wondered if they should resign as so many of the pre-war congregation were moving out of London or were called up to serve in the Armed Forces. Sunday collections no longer met the weekly expenses and the salaries of both men were cut drastically. Campbell Morgan feared that he had influenced his younger colleague wrongly but these fears did not shake Martyn's strong conviction that his coming to Westminster was right.

The 'phoney war' when many in Britain, including the Lloyd-Jones family, thought hostilities would end within a year, soon gave way in 1940 to Dunkirk, the Battle of Britain and the incessant bombing of British cities. The Germans began dropping incendiary bombs in September 1940. One of them hit the Chapel but with no serious damage.

Being so close to Buckingham Palace and Wellington barracks, Campbell Morgan felt the Chapel was in a dangerous position so he moved Sunday worship for a time

Facing page: Westminster Chapel in Campbell Morgan's time

Above: Campbell Morgan preaching at Westminster Chapel to a congregation of nearly 2,000 in the 1930s Facing page: view from the pulpit, 1930s

Westminster Chapel

In 1744, the Countess of Huntingdon took over an influential Nonconformist place of worship in Westminster, called 'Princess Street Chapel' and renamed it 'Westminster Chapel'. It could accommodate 3,000 people. What connection this chapel had with the present one remains uncertain. The first Westminster Chapel at Buckingham Gate was opened for worship on 6 May 1841 with twenty-two members. The following year they called a minister, Samuel Martin, who served for 35 years. Such was the success of his labours that the chapel, seating 1,500, was pulled down to be replaced in 1865 by the present building designed to hold 2,500. Almost encircling the entire building are two galleries, one above the other, but designed as not to overshadow those below. From almost every seat the central pulpit, replaced during Morgan's first pastorate by a large circular rostrum, is clearly visible. At the rear of the church building there is a large ground floor hall and an equally large first floor area, known as the Institute Hall but now named after Lloyd-Jones.

to a nearby hall that had better facilities for war-time conditions. But Lloyd-Jones encouraged Morgan and the members to return to the Chapel where they continued to worship for most of the war. During 1941 the Chapel was hit three times, but the night fire-fighters on the premises saved the building from going up in flames.

Lloyd-Jones carried on his ministry as normal, preaching in different parts of England and alternating, morning or evening with Campbell Morgan at the Chapel. One weekend in May 1941 he was preaching at Mansfield College Chapel, Oxford, on the Sunday morning. He was due to return by train that same day to minister at Westminster Chapel but the Principal of the College informed him that Westminster was ablaze after heavy bombing during the night and suggested he had better remain in Oxford and preach for them in the evening. However, Lloyd-Jones was determined to get back, believing that all would be well.

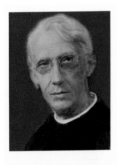

G. Campbell Morgan (1863–1945)

Rejected by the Wesleyan Methodists when he was twenty-five because he lacked academic qualifications, he was ordained by the Congregationalists in 1889 and pastored churches in Staffordshire and North London. The American evangelist, D.L. Moody, invited him to preach in North America and after Moody's death in 1899 Morgan accepted the challenge to become a Bible lecturer at Moody's centre. He was first called to Westminster Chapel in 1904. Under Campbell Morgan, congregations increased from 200 to nearly 2,000. He was also appointed President of the Cheshunt Congregational College, Cambridge. Morgan resigned from the Chapel in 1917 and again moved to the States where he engaged in a most fruitful itinerant ministry before becoming pastor of Tabernacle Presbyterian Church, Philadelphia. In his seventieth year, Morgan returned to Britain to assist Dr Simpson at Westminster Chapel and when the latter resigned through ill health, he became the minister for the second time in 1935. He retired in 1943 and died two years later. Lloyd-Jones preached the sermon at his memorial service.

Top: *Statue of Winston Churchill facing the Houses of Parliament*

Above: *18 Chatsworth Avenue, Haslemere where the family lived for four years during the war. It was a newly built house which they rented and Lloyd-Jones gave it the name 'Haven'*

Above, lower: *Haslemere today*

At Paddington station he eventually got a taxi, although the driver was dubious about getting through to the Chapel because well-known places like Westminster School, Westminster Abbey and the Houses of Parliament had been hit. However, by using the back streets they eventually found Westminster Chapel unscathed. What is more, people had gathered for the evening worship so he was able to preach as usual.

During the early days of the war, Lloyd-Jones preached a series of five sermons that were immediately put into print by Hodder and Stoughton at the close of 1939. The book was entitled, *Why does God allow war?* In it he questioned people's motives in praying for peace: 'Have we a right to expect God to preserve a state of peace merely to allow men and women to continue a life that is an insult to His holy Name?' At the same time he encouraged them to submit to God, to trust Christ and to take hold of the divine promises.

Tranquil in trouble

His own life of quiet confidence in God in those critical days of the war was a wonderful example of what he was preaching. In December 1939 Bethan and the girls returned from West Wales where they had moved for safety at the beginning of the war, to rented accommodation in Haslemere, Surrey. From here Martyn would journey to London and other places to preach. Towards the close of 1943, thinking that the worst of the war was over, the family rented

Above: Buckingham Palace from St James' Park

a house at 2 Colebrooke Avenue, Ealing, North London. But in June 1944, when Londoners were beginning to relax, came the deadly attacks by the V1 flying bombs, called 'doodle-bugs'. Houses near the Lloyd-Jones' home were hit. By the end of July 1944, nearly 5,000 people had been killed and hundreds of buildings destroyed.

In June 1944 one 'doodle-bug' landed on the Guards Chapel at the Wellington barracks killing over 120 people and injuring hundreds more as they met for Sunday worship. This was only a few hundred yards from Westminster Chapel. At the time, Lloyd-Jones was in the middle of his prayer when the menacing sound of the bomb was heard overhead and then silence as the engine cut out. The congregation rose to its feet at the sound of the blast and the church building shook. After a brief pause, the preacher continued his prayer as though nothing had happened and the congregation sat down again. Lloyd-Jones was covered in white dust from the Chapel ceiling but after he had been dusted down by the secretary the service continued.

The following month a bomb fell even closer, on the flats opposite the Chapel in Castle Street. It blew half the Chapel roof off but amazingly the interior was undamaged. The congregation, now reduced to about 150, moved into the borrowed hall again. It took fourteen weeks to repair the damage. Elizabeth, Lloyd-Jones' elder daughter, then in her teens, recalls how the congregation was small in number 'and the sense of danger from the unpredictable bombs was ever present. But our sense of fellowship was very strong, and…we still knew the presence of the glory of the Lord.'

Creating a church fellowship

Despite the loss of Campbell Morgan's great congregation, the war brought new faces to the Chapel. Many members of the Allied forces attended and when hostilities finally ceased, these people went back to places as far apart as New Zealand and the United States spreading the word of this man's amazing ministry in the centre of London.

From the beginning of the 20th century the Chapel had become a preaching centre, with little in the way of spiritual fellowship among the members. It concerned Lloyd-Jones that people did not know one another and the spiritual life of the church was weak. With the support of Campbell Morgan, he established a weekly prayer meeting which was held prior to the evening service. Later, an additional prayer meeting was held on Wednesday evenings.

When Morgan retired, Lloyd-Jones replaced the Friday Bible Class with a Fellowship meeting, like the one he had introduced at Sandfields, where people were allowed to raise questions that were then opened up for discussion. Besides getting everyone to think biblically, it strengthened the fellowship and people became less reserved. Instead of members' meetings being formal, short sessions, he arranged for missionaries to speak after the business of the church had been completed. Informal 'At Home' meetings were introduced after the summer breaks and members and friends of Westminster Chapel came to look forward eagerly to these occasions when he and Bethan Lloyd-Jones would chat to everyone in turn over tea. Lloyd-

Facing page: On June 18, 1944 a German V-1 hit the Royal Military Chapel, Wellington Barracks, killing 58 civilians and 63 service personnel

Right: Martyn and Bethan in their early 50s

Facing page inset: Westminster Chapel in the 1940s

Jones would then give an informative, often humorous, account of their summer holidays before sending them away with words that did not fail to encourage all present. At the beginning of each New Year, he would send out a letter to the members highlighting Chapel concerns and invariably urging closer relationships.

Members of the congregation were encouraged to stay for the whole of Sunday. Food was often shared with visitors. This was the church family at its best: talking, sharing concerns and ideas, and supporting the whole work. The Sunday School and Bible Classes took place in the afternoon before they had tea together, which was followed by a time of prayer before the evening service.

Lloyd-Jones was always available after each of the services on Sundays and on Friday evenings to counsel those with pastoral concerns. With his experience as a doctor he was able to detect those in genuine need and to give time to them, while graciously directing others to the door after a few minutes conversation. He regularly helped not only members of his congregation but students, fellow ministers, and vast numbers of missionaries on home assignments, and visitors from overseas. If they came with a measure of trepidation after seeing the rather austere figure in the pulpit, they were soon put at ease and went away conscious they had been in the presence of a very kindly person.

When he came to retire from Westminster Chapel he sent a letter to each member in which the pastoral heart of the preacher was clearly evident. It included the following paragraph: 'What things we have experienced! To a preacher nothing is so wonderful as to feel the unction of the Holy Spirit while preaching, and to hear of souls being brought under conviction of sin, and then experiencing the new birth. Thank

God, that has often been our experience. But not only that, one remembers marriages, births, deaths, even war and bombing … faced together; but above all I shall treasure the privilege of ministering to those with grievous problems of various types and enjoying the trust and confidence of those passing through dark and deep waters.'

Expansion

Towards the end of the war, some of the members and deacons doubted whether the plain services, without a choir and organ recital, would attract people back to the Chapel. But by 1948 the first gallery was again opened. During the Festival of Britain centenary exhibition in 1951 when throngs of people visited London, the second gallery came into use and the Chapel was at times completely full.

His Friday evening fellowship meetings finally ended in 1952. They were replaced by a series of addresses on Christian doctrine. Numbers so increased that they moved from the hall into the main Chapel building. He began his great series of expository sermons on Paul's Letter to the Romans in 1955. Thirteen years later, when he retired, he still had over two more chapters to expound. Some

Left: A cartoon picture of Lloyd-Jones one Friday evening in the early 1960s. Responding to someone in the congregation, the Doctor replied, 'My friend—such a thesis is utterly and entirely insupportable, you listen to what Paul says…'

Right: Lloyd-Jones preaching at Westminster Chapel in the early 1960s

of these sermons were printed during his retirement but most have been published since his death.

Students from all parts of the world were gripped by his preaching. Doctors and nurses attended in large numbers. Scientists and theologians, servants to the royal household, members of both houses of Parliament were to be found among the congregation. People who later became influential in their own countries have testified to the spiritual benefit they received from the powerful messages. One was a Lt Colonel in the Ghanaian armed forces while another became the president of Kenya.

Lloyd-Jones developed a pattern of preaching more pastorally on Sunday mornings and strongly evangelistic messages on Sunday evenings. The Friday night meetings grounded people in the great doctrines of the Christian Faith with practical application. His sermons could be understood by everyone. Children and young people, those with little education as well as university dons, were gripped and made to consider eternal issues.

The Chapel services

There was a sense of expectancy, even excitement, as the congregation gathered. Unlike Campbell Morgan who was tall and elegant, Lloyd-Jones was short and slim. He would appear in the pulpit wearing a black Geneva gown that covered his dark three-piece suit. After bowing his head briefly in prayer the service would begin. Lloyd-Jones led the people, through his prayers, into the presence of God and then preached from the Bible passage in such a way that it was

as if they were directly hearing the voice of God. One student from Jamaica spoke for many: 'It was as if I lost all count of time and space. The eternal truth that I hungered for so deeply was being revealed, and I was caught up body, mind and spirit in the sublime experience of receiving, finding, understanding, knowing.'

His concern for a revival of spiritual life in the church as experienced in the 18th century, has been taken as his one great obsession. Such language is inappropriate when we consider the various organizations with which he was involved and his own activity in seeking to spread the gospel. But his view of revival should be seen as an important factor in keeping him from the excesses of the Pentecostal and charismatic movements on the one hand and from a cold non-emotional Calvinism on the other. During the centenary of the 1859 revival he preached a series of sermons on revival that encouraged Christians to look to God and not human ingenuity for seasons of blessing. Lloyd-Jones emphasised that only an unusual work of the Spirit in the church could alter the general spiritual state of the British people. His view of the baptism of the Spirit was to be understood in this

Above: The palace of Westminster and Westminster bridge

Facing page, top: Path to the Brynuchaf farm of John and Mari Jones at Llanymawddwy.

Facing page, inset: Taken in the 1960s, the picture shows Lloyd-Jones and his wife with Elizabeth Braund and a group of inner city young people on holiday at the farm belonging to John and Mari Jones in Llanymawddwy

context, and on several occasions he himself had known overwhelming experiences of God's love giving assurances of salvation and power to witness.

That his prayers could be as powerfully used as his preaching is shown from an incident that happened during the 1950s. A professing Christian, who had left his wife and family in Wales to live with another woman in London, and who had lied to his wife to obtain money from her, had ended up destitute and lonely. One Sunday afternoon he resolved to commit suicide by throwing himself off Westminster bridge into the Thames. As he was nearing the Houses of Parliament, suddenly Big Ben struck 6.30 and he remembered that Lloyd-Jones would be about to commence the service at Westminster Chapel. He decided to go for the last time and listen to the preacher he had heard many years before in South Wales. He arrived at the Chapel as Lloyd-Jones was leading the people in prayer. The first words he heard were, 'God have mercy upon the backslider'. Immediately the man was convicted and he eventually returned to his wife and became an active worker in a local church.

Elizabeth Braund, a script writer for the BBC, was one of the converts of the 1950s. She was a non-churchgoer who was invited to attend an evening service by one

Left: Llanymawddwy Welsh Congregational Chapel—one of the last places where Lloyd-Jones preached in Wales

Below: The hills surrounding Brynuchaf farm, Llanymawddwy

of the Chapel members. In 1959 she was involved in the launch of the Evangelical Magazine, but it was with her unique work among the young people of South London, near Clapham Junction, that she has been more commonly associated. In this she had the sympathetic ear and support of Martyn and Bethan Lloyd-Jones. For a number of years she took a group of inner city boys on a camping holiday in the mountains of North Wales. They stayed on a farm in Llanymawddwy with friends of the Lloyd-Joneses. One summer when the minister of Westminster Chapel and his wife were guests in the farmhouse, Lloyd-Jones preached on Sunday in English to these boys in the little Welsh chapel. One lad commented, ''E's all right, that bloke. I could understand wot 'e said'.

Westminster Chapel, Buckingham Gate SW1

Nearest underground is St James Park (Circle, District). Buses 11,24,211 stop in Victoria Street near Buckingham Gate. Chapel office ☎ 02078341731.

Buckingham Palace

On the site of Buckingham House, George IV commissioned the building of the present 600 room Palace soon after his accession in 1820, but it was not finished until Queen Victoria's time. The present Queen and the Duke of Edinburgh have a suite of rooms on the first floor of the north wing and on the south side is the Queen's gallery. When the Queen is in residence

Above: Facing Buckingham Palace, the Victoria Memorial is an imposing, tall edifice by the sculptor Thomas Brock (1911)

her personal flag, the royal Standard, flies from the palace mast. The changing of the guard ceremony takes place in the palace forecourt most mornings. Nearest underground is St James' Park (Circle, District).

The Queen's Gallery is open to the public. For

tickets and information ☎ 02077992331; E-mail: information@royalcollection.org.uk

For the Royal Mews ☎ 02077667302 or see www.royal.gov.uk

St James' Palace

Henry VIII had this palace built on the site of St James' Hospital for leper women and it became one of the principal royal residences in London. This is where his daughter, Queen Mary, died, where Elizabeth and James I held court, and where Charles I spent his last night before his execution at Whitehall. In 1809 much of it was destroyed by fire but afterwards restored. Here also Queen Victoria and the future George V were both married. The accession of a new sovereign is still proclaimed here.

Blewcoat School

St James' Park

This is the oldest of London's royal parks, named after St James' Hospital, and is home to over thirty species of birds.

Lancaster House

Originally called York House to accommodate the Duke of York during the reign of George IV, it is now the venue for the meetings of the Commonwealth Heads of State.

Clarence House

Built by George IV to provide a house for the Duke of Clarence, later to become William IV. This is where Queen Elizabeth the Queen Mother lived after the death of her husband, George VI. Prince Charles and his sons now reside here and some of the rooms are open to the public.

Green Park

The area is said to be the burial ground of the lepers from St James' Hospital. Charles II made it into a royal park. At one time it was frequented by highwaymen. Handel composed music for a firework display here in 1748.

The Mall

Created by Charles II to replace Pall Mall as the alley for playing a French nobleman's game with a wooden hammer and ball. It also became a fashionable promenade. As a memorial to Queen Victoria the Mall was altered in 1904 and became a royal processional route linking the Queen Victoria memorial in front of Buckingham Palace with Admiralty Arch.

Birdcage Walk

The site of James I's aviary which his grandson Charles II enlarged. Up to 1828 only the Grand Falconer and the royal family could drive down it.

Wellington Barracks

The barracks between Birdcage Walk and Petty France was once associated with the Foot Guards. The present Guards Chapel contains a monument to those who were killed by the bomb that destroyed the original chapel in 1944. There is also a museum.

Blewcoat School, Caxton Street, SW1

It was founded in about 1688 to provide an education for children from the slums around Westminster Abbey. The building dates from 1709 and was used as a school until 1939. In 1954 it was bought by the National Trust. The statue over the doorway is of a charity boy in his blue coat. The Street takes its name from William Caxton who set up his printing press at Westminster in the 1470s—a development that would aid the spread of the English Bible.

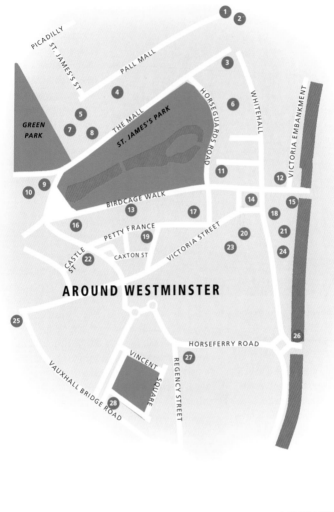

KEY

1 TRAFALGAR SQ

2 CHARLES I STATUE

3 ADMIRALTY ARCH

4 MARLBOROUGH HOUSE

5 ST. JAMES'S PALACE

6 HORSEGUARDS PARADE

7 LANCASTER HOUSE

8 CLARENCE HOUSE

9 QN. VICTORIA MEMORIAL

10 BUCKINGHAM PALACE

11 CABINET WAR ROOMS

12 WESTMINSTER TUBE STN.

13 GUARDS' CHAPEL

14 CHURCHILL STATUE

15 WESTMINSTER BRIDGE

16 WELLINGTON BARRACKS

17 METHODIST CENTRAL HALL

18 CROMWELL STATUE

19 ST. JAMES'S PK TUBE STN.

20 ST.MARGARET'S WESTMINSTER

21 WESTMINSTER HALL

22 WESTMINSTER CHAPEL

23 WESTMINSTER ABBEY

24 HOUSES OF PARLIAMENT

25 VICTORIA RAIL AND TUBE

26 LAMBETH BRIDGE

27 NO.7 REGENCY ST.

28 NO.12 VINCENT SQ

Above: Westminister Abbey

have been associated with the Hall. In 1946 the inaugural meeting of the General Assembly of the United Nations was held here when the Secretary General and members of the Security Council were elected. Nearest underground station is Westminster (Circle, District, Jubilee). Bus services 11, 24, 211 stop nearby.

Westminister Abbey

From the time of the Coronation of William the Conqueror on Christmas Day 1066, most English monarchs have been crowned here. Many famous people are buried here and on 1 July 1643 the *Westmintser Confession of Faith* was signed.

Parliament Square

Slums around the area were cleared in 1868 to make way for this more suitable approach to the Houses of Parliament. Among the statues of statesmen and soldiers in the square is one of

Winston Churchill.

Nearest underground is Westminster (Circle, District, Victoria). Bus services 3, 11, 12, 24, 53, 159, 211 stop nearby.

Methodist Central Hall, Westminster (see next chapter)

Opened in 1912 as a monument to mark the centenary of John Wesley's death. The building is Viennese Baroque in style with Romanesque decoration. The Great Hall with its impressive dome seats 2,350. Preachers such as Dynsdale Young and W.E. Sangster ministered here. More recently the Lloyd-Webbers

Whitehall

Now occupied by government offices. Statues of Oliver Cromwell and Richard I are at one end of Whitehall, and Charles I at the other. The statue of Richard I occupies the site where Guy Fawkes and three fellow conspirators were executed in January 1606, in the shadow of the building they had tried to blow up.

Westminster Hall

Begun in 1097 this is almost all that remains of the Palace of Westminster where many state trials have taken place including those of Sir Thomas More in 1535, Anne Boleyn in 1536 and Charles I in 1649. At various times it has been the seat of government and housed the law courts. It is now the vestibule of the House of Commons.

39 MOUNT PARK
CRESCENT WHERE THE
LLOYD-JONES FAMILY
MOVED IN JULY 1945

EALING

KEY

1 NO. 2 COLEBROOKE AVENUE

2 NO. 39 MOUNT PARK CRESCENT

3 NO. 49 CREFFIELD ROAD

St Margaret's Church, Westminster

Standing in the shadow of Westminster Abbey. In 1614 when members of Parliament wished to dissociate themselves from High Church practices associated with the Abbey next door, they decided to worship separately in this parish church that once served most of the city of Westminster. Ever since, it has been the parish church of the House of Commons. The Commons adjourned business to give thanks for victory and peace in 1918 and 1945. The original church was built about 1066. It was enlarged in the 14th century. The present building took 35 years to build and was finished in 1523. Milton, Pepys, Churchill and Margaret Thatcher were all married here. More significantly, the Puritans John Owen and Richard Baxter preached here. In front of the West Door is a flat slab with the initials TR on it; this is a Roman milestone or boundary stone.

LET THE PEOPLE PRAISE THEE O GOD

Above: Big Ben, the 320 foot high Clock Tower is named after the largest bell, weighing over 13 tons

7 Influence and Isolation

From the forties to 'the swinging sixties' Lloyd-Jones was the most significant person in British evangelicalism. He also became a controversial figure and this lead to a loss of influence and popularity in some quarters

Lloyd-Jones came to London at a time when there was a vacuum in the leadership of the Nonconformist (non-Anglican) denominations which made up the Free Church Federal Council. The father figure of the Free Churches, J. D. Jones of Bournemouth, pleaded with him to take on the position of leadership. It was a tempting proposition at a time when Lloyd-Jones saw a dramatic fall in numbers at Westminster Chapel but he knew it would mean compromising his evangelical convictions.

Throughout the country Lloyd-Jones was seen primarily as an evangelist and there were few evangelistic campaigns of any size planned during the 1940s without him being either consulted or invited to preach. A Free Church Council spokesman hailed him as 'the modern Moody' (the American evangelist who had held numerous missions in Britain in the 19th century).

Lloyd-Jones preached in all the great auditoriums of the country. In December 1935 he first spoke in the Royal Albert Hall, London, at a Bible Witness Rally, and when an evangelistic campaign was held there in 1945 Lloyd-Jones preached at one of the meetings. He was again at the Albert Hall in

Above: *Lloyd-Jones preaching to a packed Albert Hall in 1935*

Facing page: *The Royal Albert Hall*

Facing page: The Usher Hall, *Edinburgh*

Above: *Lloyd-Jones preaching at St Andrew's Hall, Glasgow*

Top: *Lloyd-Jones preaching to a congregation of 4,000 at the Kelvin Hall, Glasgow in 1963*

Facing page, **bottom:** *Memorial to the Aberfan victims*

1961 at the invitation of the Evangelical Alliance when a rally was held to commemorate the 350th anniversary of the Authorised Version of the Bible. The place was packed with 8,000 people. This writer was present as a teenager in the top gallery. His reading from the Bible was in itself powerful and the preaching that followed was such that time stood still and the message made an indelible impression on my life.

In April 1939 at the Usher Hall, the largest in Edinburgh, Lloyd-Jones was the main speaker at a week long united mission. When he spoke in the great St Andrew's Hall, Glasgow, in 1942, the newspapers reported that it was one of the largest gatherings of its kind ever seen in the city, with over a thousand people being turned away. In Belfast in January 1966, he spoke at the first public meeting of the Evangelical Fellowship of Ireland in the large Wellington Hall when, even with the provision of an overflow venue, hundreds were turned away. He also preached to 4,000 people on numerous occasions in the Free Trade Hall, Manchester.

Later in his ministry, it was to Lloyd-Jones that the people of Aberfan turned on the first anniversary of the devastating disaster that hit the place. In this tight-knit South Wales mining community near Merthyr Tydfil on 21 October 1966, a coal waste tip slipped and engulfed the primary school killing altogether in the village 116 children and 28 adults. A whole generation of youngsters with their teachers was wiped out. All the denominations

gathered at the Presbyterian Chapel for an afternoon and evening service on 15 November 1967 with the evening service relayed to another packed chapel across the road. His evening text was Romans 8:18–23, 'For I reckon that the sufferings of this present time are not worthy to be compared with the glory which shall be revealed in us ...' A local Anglican vicar commented on the moving and uplifting nature of the sermon. It did not consist in trite platitudes but in a well-reasoned and authoritative presentation of the Christian message that brought comfort and hope to a bewildered people.

Encouraging evangelical organizations

Lloyd-Jones did not initiate any new organization or society and it was often only through the persuasion of others that he became involved. The general secretary of the Inter-Varsity Fellowship (IVF) gained his confidence and for a number of years Lloyd-Jones served as its President. His input at committee meetings and addresses at conferences raised the profile of this student work making it more theologically robust. He was involved in setting up what eventually emerged as the Tyndale Fellowship for Biblical Research. Other affiliated arms of the IVF, now called UCCF (Universities and Colleges Christian Fellowship) in which Lloyd-Jones played a substantial part in their formation and early development were the Graduates Fellowship, the Theological Students Fellowship (TSF), the Christian Medical Fellowship (CMF), and the International Fellowship of Evangelical Students (IFES).

Lloyd-Jones took part in university missions, particularly during his early years at Westminster. In 1941 he was invited to preach in Oxford with other well-known speakers like William Temple who later became  Archbishop of Canterbury. On his first Sunday evening at the university, Lloyd-Jones preached from the pulpit of St Mary's. Afterwards, the vicar allowed questions and one undergraduate asked why the preacher had given them a sermon that could equally well have been delivered to a congregation of farm labourers. After a roar of laughter, Lloyd-Jones replied that he could not understand the questioner's difficulty, as he had always regarded undergraduates and indeed all the members of Oxford University 'as being just ordinary common clay and miserable sinners like everyone else' and that 'their needs were precisely the same as those of the agricultural labourers or anyone else.'

Among those present and converted at a mission arranged by the London Inter-Faculty Christian Unions and lead by Lloyd-Jones in 1947, was Professor R.V.G. Tasker, head of the New Testament Department at King's College and one of the men involved in the New English Bible translation. When the IVF Easter Conferences met at Trinity College, Cambridge, in 1941 and

Above: Bala lake

Top: *Tyndale House, Selwyn Gardens, Cambridge, the home of the Tyndale Fellowship with its extensive library for biblical research*

Left, top: Bryn–y-groes, Bala, *where the Welsh Ministers Conference has been held since 1961*

Left, lower: Lloyd-Jones *with some Welsh ministers in the mid-1960s*

1942, the Master of Trinity, the eminent historian, G.M. Trevelyan, heard him preach. On the second occasion he was visibly moved and came up to Lloyd-Jones commenting, 'Sir, it has been given to you to speak with great power'.

In 1934 at the Westminster Central Hall, London, Martyn was invited to speak for the first time at the Annual Meeting of the China Inland Mission (CIM; later renamed Overseas Missionary Fellowship). Almost twenty years later, when Fred Mitchell, the Home Director of CIM and chairman of the Keswick Convention, was killed in a Comet air disaster over India, it was Lloyd-Jones who was asked to preside and preach at the Memorial Service.

His influence spread to other major organizations including the Children's Special Service Mission (CSSM), Scripture Union (SU), and the Crusaders' Union. To the leaders of this latter group in 1942, he delivered an address on evangelism that spelt out much of the thinking that lay behind his own evangelistic work. It was published under the title *The Presentation of the Gospel*.

The Evangelical Movement of Wales (EMW) owes a great deal to the influence of 'Dr Martyn' as he was often called in the land of his birth. This Movement arose out of the Welsh student work in which he was closely involved during its early years. Unless prevented through sickness or absence overseas, Lloyd-Jones attended all the annual EMW Ministers' Conferences until his final illness in 1979.

Left: A light-hearted moment on the Areopagus (Mars Hill), Athens during his visit to Greece with Bethan and Ann in August 1961. The pastor of the evangelical church at Katerini was greatly influenced by Lloyd-Jones' preaching at Westminster and a former member of the Chapel later went out to assist the Greek pastor

Overseas engagements took him to many places in Europe and North America. He also made one visit to South Africa in 1958. During the summer of 1957, he stayed in Switzerland with Francis and Edith Schaeffer who had recently set up the L'Abri Fellowship, and Martyn spoke at their daughter's wedding.

Promoting Puritan spirituality

It was through the involvement of Lloyd-Jones that the Evangelical Library was housed in the heart of London in 1945. He made great use of the place himself and encouraged others to read the works of John Calvin, the Puritans and Jonathan Edwards, the 18th century preacher and theologian of New England. It was with the aim of republishing books of this nature that *The Banner of Truth Trust* was set up in 1955 with the enthusiastic support of Lloyd-Jones. (For 'the Puritans' see *Travel with John Bunyan* pp. 14–15 and for 'Calvin' see *Travel with C.H.Spurgeon* p. 79 both in this series.)

The Puritan Conference came into being through the influence of the preaching of Lloyd-Jones on several Oxford undergraduates. Among them was Jim Packer, who has become one of the most able theologians of the 20th century. Another Oxford student, Raymond Johnston, who later organized *The Festival of Light* (now known as *Care Trust*) seems to have been the one to put the idea of a Puritan Conference into Lloyd-Jones' mind. The first was held at Westminster Chapel in

Above: *The Evangelical Library Chilton Street, London*

Facing page: *Francis Schaeffer (1912–1984), an American Christian apologist of German ancestry, who influenced many students at his Swiss home, L'Abri, and through his talks and writings, helping them to see that God exists and giving them a biblical base from which to attack secular culture*

December 1950. Packer did the organising and Lloyd-Jones chaired the sessions. It became a tradition for Lloyd-Jones to give the closing address. These discourses not only indicated considerable historical research, but they sent people away freshly challenged to live godly lives and to reform church life in the light of the Bible.

Caring for Christian leaders

Out of a small private gathering of Christian leaders there emerged The Westminster Fellowship which began meeting quarterly on Tuesday mornings at Westminster Chapel from 1941 onwards. Lloyd-Jones was asked to chair these meetings and the Fellowship soon increased in numbers with pastors attending from as far away as the West Country, the Midlands, Wales, the North of England and East Anglia. Eventually up to 400 ministers met on the first Monday of every month in the Institute Hall to learn from 'The Doctor', as he was affectionately called. In the morning, a question of a theological nature would be raised from the floor and he would guide the discussion and close the session by summing up the conclusions in a masterly way. The afternoon session was given over to pastoral concerns. On each occasion he would encourage the participants to think, and to think biblically, and he always sent the men away challenged and stimulated to action. When he was asked, one afternoon, what he thought about acupuncture, the Doctor amazed everyone for the next hour with an impromptu informative address that helped everyone to understand and evaluate the subject. The Westminster Fellowship proved to be one of Lloyd-Jones' most influential ministries to pastors. What many had lacked in their ministerial training they gained from this in-service training, or 'finishing school for ministers', as one pastor has called it. The meeting was a high priority in his

Above: A group photograph at the second Banner of Truth Ministers' Conference in Leicester, July 1964, with Lloyd-Jones and Professor John Murray of Westminster Theological Seminary, USA, who were the two main speakers

diary and the Doctor would always be back for it, wherever he had been preaching on Sunday.

Lloyd-Jones was instrumental in the formation of two colleges, the London Bible College (LBC) and the London Theological Seminary (LTS). Concerning the former, such was the respect in which Lloyd-Jones was held that an invitation was given to him in 1942 to become Principal of the proposed college. He declined but worked with the committee, becoming Vice-Chairman in 1943. It was he who suggested the name of Ernest Kevan, a Baptist pastor who eventually became the first Principal of LBC.

Lloyd-Jones' theological influence

When Lloyd-Jones became a preacher, Christianity in Britain was far too superficial and mindless and he observed that there was some truth in the charge that religion was nothing but 'the opiate of the people'. He therefore encouraged a new generation to use their minds, teaching them to think biblically and not like the rationalists who ignored the spiritual dimension. Theology was often distrusted or even despised among evangelicals but he encouraged, particularly through his own preaching, an interest in theology that was 'Reformed' but not speculative and philosophical. Reformed Theology is that brand of Protestantism that is Calvinistic in doctrine and practice. The type of Reformed Theology he embraced was in the tradition of 17th century British Puritanism and the 18th century Calvinistic Methodists which was never dry and academic, but warm, practical and spiritually helpful.

It was through his influence that evangelical scholarship began to flourish again in the United Kingdom and Evangelical Calvinistic theology has spread to all parts of the world. One of the leading New Testament scholars of today, N T Wright, the newly installed bishop of Durham, has expressed his own appreciation of Lloyd-Jones' sermons on Romans, describing them as a 'remarkable series'. He draws attention to the achievement of Lloyd-Jones in emphasizing the implications of the Christian's union with Christ.

Above: The old London Bible College building on Marylebone Road now Heron House. The foundation stone reads 'This stone laid to the glory of God 30th May 1957 "Thy Word is Truth"'

Church unity

In the immediate post-war years it was Lloyd-Jones' influence that strengthened the biblical convictions of the leadership within the Evangelical Alliance (EA), as a later secretary of the Alliance admitted, and he was often asked to speak at their meetings. Unlike many in the EA, however, Lloyd-Jones did not support the methods of modern evangelism, especially the 'appeals' or 'altar calls'. He was similarly unhappy at the way the Billy Graham Crusades encouraged sponsorship from clergymen who were liberal in their views of the Bible and from leaders within Roman Catholicism.

Lloyd-Jones first met Billy Graham at a Conference in the States in 1956 where they were both speaking. When Graham held his first Crusade in London, Lloyd-Jones refused to be critical but he did not participate. The influence of Lloyd-Jones was such that Graham called on him in 1963 to invite him to be the chairman at the first 'World Congress on Evangelism' that eventually took place in Berlin. Lloyd-Jones indicated that if Graham would stop having liberal and Roman Catholic clergymen on his campaign platforms and would drop the invitation system then he would wholeheartedly support him and chair the congress. They talked for three hours but Graham could not accept the conditions. Respect for each other continued,

Left: *Central Hall, Westminster*

Facing page: *Lloyd-Jones with some Methodist ministers in the late 1950s. To the right of Lloyd-Jones is Charles Lawrence who seceded from the denomination*

and when the evangelist was suffering from a potentially serious throat problem, Lloyd-Jones introduced him to a medical friend who was a specialist.

As a result of the 1954–55 Graham crusades, the British Council of Churches (BCC) initiated discussions with evangelicals on co-operation in evangelism. Lloyd-Jones accepted the invitation to be part of the consultation committee and he attended regularly from November 1956 until it disbanded in April 1961. Interest waned when it was clear that there was no unity among the participants concerning the central truths of the Christian faith. As Lloyd-Jones stated later: 'We had demonstrated that no co-operation was possible.'

When in 1964 the BCC committed itself to 'one Church' not later than Easter 1980, Lloyd-Jones, who had already been promoting unity among evangelicals, encouraged his friends in the traditional denominations to consider the possibility of coming together in some kind of visible church unity to counteract the all-inclusive type of unity envisaged by the ecumenical movement. Instead of them being content to express their unity in evangelical societies outside their church affiliations he urged that they should indicate their spiritual unity in a much more biblical way. In their organisations evangelicals were careful not to admit non-evangelicals and yet in church life they were prepared to work with people who denied the basic statements of the Creed. He argued that it was not schism to separate from such people because their beliefs clearly showed they were not Christian; he believed that in reality what was sinful and schismatic was for evangelical

people to be divided from one another in their various denominational groupings.

Lloyd-Jones has been accused of dividing evangelicals in the United Kingdom. This is a superficial understanding of the aftermath of his controversial address in 1966 at the Second National Assembly of Evangelicals in the Westminster Central Hall. The sad fact was that too many evangelicals were more attached to their denominations than to working for evangelical church unity. The reports of this address in the Christian media were at best misleading and failed to pick up on the essence of his message. One religious correspondent claimed that Lloyd-Jones had made 'an eloquent plea to evangelicals to leave their denominations and join a United Evangelical Church'. He had never said anything about a 'United Evangelical Church'—it

was, in fact, the Evangelical Alliance that had set up a Commission to study such a possibility.

Lloyd-Jones argued that if non-evangelicals realised that visible disunity among Christians was sinful, should evangelicals who made much of their spiritual unity be content to allow it to be distorted through their close associations with those who ignored or denied the gospel truths?

He appealed to his audience: 'Do we not feel the call to come together, not occasionally, but *always*? It is a grief to me that I spend so little of my time with some of my brethren…I am a believer in ecumenicity, evangelical ecumenicity. To me, the tragedy is that we are divided…' He did not underestimate the problems of acting on his call, but he considered it to be 'a day of

Above: Lloyd-Jones talking to John Stott after the Evangelical Alliance meeting on 18 October 1966

glorious opportunity'. He was not calling for a united evangelical church on denominational lines, but an association or federation of churches and evangelical denominations with a minimum of central control. The details would have to be worked out but he wanted people to grasp the principle and act upon it.

So compelling was the reasoning and power with which he delivered his address that the chairman, John Stott, rector of All Souls Langham Place, near Oxford Circus, dampened the highly charged atmosphere by flatly contradicting the preacher's thesis. He was afraid that ministers would be stirred to leave their denominations on mass. Stott afterwards apologised privately to Lloyd-Jones for his discourteous behaviour, but this was not made public at the time.

It was a missed opportunity and the blame clearly lay at the feet of the denominationally-minded leaders. As a result of the meeting and the compromises that became more evident as time progressed, there was a parting of the ways between those evangelicals who were content to remain in their denominations at any cost and those who came out or remained in with a reluctant spirit. The Westminster Fellowship was now only open to the second group and Lloyd-Jones' close relationship with Jim Packer ended. The Puritan Conference for 1970 was cancelled and later reconstituted and given a fresh title: 'The

Left: Martyn and Bethan, 1968

Westminster Conference'. While this may have seemed to many a negative and separatist reaction, Lloyd-Jones with his pastoral wisdom knew that, without change, their former meetings for fellowship and conference would only degenerate into strife and wrangling. Nevertheless, Lloyd-Jones continued to have a great regard for men like John Stott and was saddened when evangelical scholars of the calibre of Jim Packer left for North America. He repeatedly stressed the need for humility and patience, 'for we must remember that men who are equally honest may differ'.

Continued influence

When Lloyd-Jones lost the ear of the wider evangelical constituency, represented by the Evangelical Alliance, he became more involved in the work of the British Evangelical Council (BEC) which was a body set up in 1952 to counter the BCC. It encouraged unity between the independent and denominational evangelical churches in the United Kingdom which opposed the ecumenical movement. Many future leaders within the Fellowship of Independent Evangelical Churches (FIEC) and the Evangelical Fellowship of Congregational Churches (EFCC) owed much to Lloyd-Jones' ministry and valued his support and advice. He encouraged his own church to help those who had suffered financially because of their loyalty to the 'Truth' and the contents of the following letter to a young minister who did heed his call is typical of his own personal concern: 'Dear ——, Many many thanks for your letter. I cannot tell you how glad I was to read it and to have all these details. You know the interest I have taken in you and your affairs and I have prayed for you daily throughout this crisis. Your letter therefore brought great encouragement and I do indeed rejoice with you in the goodness and graciousness of God to you. I have been wondering how I could help you. Perhaps we can talk about this sometime at the Westminster Fellowship …'

8 The Final Years

Although Martyn Lloyd-Jones spent most of his life in England, he was born in Wales, conversed in Welsh at home, preached throughout Wales often through the medium of Welsh, died on Wales' national day, and his body was laid to rest in the heart of Welsh Wales

Retirement

Friday, 1 March, 1968 was to be Martyn's final sermon from the pulpit of Westminster Chapel as the minister of the church. He was admitted to the Royal London Homoeopathic Hospital the following Thursday, where he underwent major surgery for cancer of the colon. It was a complete success and people assumed that he would return in the autumn to resume his ministry at the Chapel. Instead, Lloyd-Jones announced his retirement. In his letter to the church at the end of May, he revealed that even before the operation he believed God was indicating that this was to be the end of one ministry and the beginning of another. He told his deacons that he wanted no special farewells and no presentations. Just as he had come to Westminster with no recognition service so he wished to leave. He had always shied away from media publicity so that his resignation drew little comment from the national newspapers and even the Christian press was muted in its response.

Above: Lloyd-Jones convalescing in Llanymawddwy after his first operation in 1968

Facing page: National Library of Wales Aberystwyth, where the Dr Lloyd-Jones Papers are held. He had been present as a child to see King George V lay the foundation stone in 1911

Above: 49 Creffield Road, Ealing, the first and only home of their own which they shared with their daughter, Ann and family. They moved here in 1965 and this is where Lloyd-Jones died in 1981

Top: With the Catherwood family at Balsham, Cambridgeshire in 1976

It was a surprise to some when Lloyd-Jones indicated that he would now be able to give more time to reading! He had been an avid reader all his life and his reading was about ten years ahead of most men in the ministry. It ranged from novels to biographies and from theological works to medical journals. In so doing he kept abreast of the latest thinking and to the end was able to debate and address a variety of subjects, whether medical, social, historical or theological. But above all the Bible remained his daily food and drink.

Retirement also gave him more opportunities to be with the family. In 1954 Elizabeth had married Fred Catherwood (later knighted for his services to the government) and in 1964 they purchased Sutton Hall, the old rectory in Balsham, East Anglia. Ann got married in 1965, the year her parents moved from Mount

Park Crescent to 49 Creffield Road, Ealing. While Martyn and Bethan lived on the ground floor, Ann's family occupied the first floor. They all adored their grandfather who did not patronise them but listened sympathetically to their concerns, winning the right to guide their thinking and activities. He watched their favourite programmes, played their games and, with their grandmother, often joined them on family holidays. At the Catherwoods' home he enjoyed a game of billiards or playing croquet on the lawn.

This did not mean he had given up on the outside world. Far from it! His final years were full and fruitful. Relieved of the pressure of his responsibilities at Westminster Chapel meant that Martyn could prepare his sermons for publication. This is what many had been urging him to do for some time and although earlier

Top: Balsham village near Cambridge.

Above: Ann's children, Adam, Elizabeth and Rhiannon who lived in daily contact with their grandparents

Below: Lloyd-Jones in his late 50s trying his hand at golf on the eighteen-hole course at Rosapenna Hotel, County Donegal, Ireland which was owned by Fred Catherwood's father

Top: *Sutton Hall, Balsham, where Lloyd-Jones spent much time in his final years*

Above: *The couch where he often sat reading in the Catherwoods' home*

Facing page: *The London Theological Seminary on the site of the Kensit Memorial College. The Lloyd-Jones' library is housed there*

sermons of his had sold well, publishers were at first somewhat reticent to print long series of sermons believing the public would not be interested. They were proved wrong as the years since his death have shown. Well over sixty books and pamphlets are in print and further sermons of his are in process of publication. There are many letters of appreciation from those converted through reading his sermons, as well as from people who have found his books helpful in their Christian lives.

Lloyd-Jones continued to speak up and down the country at weeknight meetings, but now he was also able to take Sunday preaching engagements in various churches and used these occasions particularly to help and encourage younger men in their ministries. While the weeknight services still brought together crowds of people, his weekend visits showed him the true state of the church scene in Britain.

Opportunities were given him

to speak on television. His effectiveness as a broadcaster had long been recognised in Wales and one newspaper columnist in the 1930s observed that Lloyd-Jones was one of the few preachers to be 'masters of the microphone'. While BBC radio listeners in Wales heard him preach on several occasions, the English side of the British Broadcasting Corporation (BBC) put time limits on his sermons that he was unwilling to accept. He made appearances on Welsh television from the beginning of the 1960s but it was in 1970 that he began to make his mark on the English network. In the programme, 'All things considered', he debated the subject of conversion with Magnus Magnusson. One junior BBC executive was heard to say, 'Dr Lloyd-Jones speaks with divine authority, we hope to have him taking part again in our programmes'. And they did. In that same year he was on BBC television four times. He was the narrator in a BBC documentary on George Whitefield's life, entitled 'The Awakener'. The shots for the film were taken in record time and he was known to the film crew as 'the one take man'. His last appearance was in December 1972 when he was interviewed by Joan Bakewell. She revealed afterwards to him that while all the clerics she had previously interviewed had assured her she was a Christian, he had been the first to tell her what she knew was her true state.

A year after his major operation for cancer, Martyn travelled with his wife to the United States. It was to be his last and longest visit and the first time they had gone by air. He had been invited by Westminster Seminary, Philadephia, to give a series of sixteen lectures to the students on 'Preaching and Preachers'. These lectures were later published in a book and have proved to be very influential across the world.

He continued to show a lively interest in the student world. It is significant that his last trip

outside the United Kingdom was to Austria in 1971 when he addressed the International Fellowship of Evangelical Students (IFES) on the subject: 'What is an Evangelical?'

Although he ministered so close to Buckingham Palace, and despite his former associations with royalty, only once was he introduced to the Queen. It took place at the British Homoeopathic Congress, when one of the long-standing members of Westminster Chapel, Dr Margery Blackie, the Queen's physician, presented the diffident Doctor to Her Majesty. On Dr Blackie's retirement, he was instrumental in the appointment of her successor. When James Callaghan, the Labour Prime Minister from 1976–79, offered him a CBE (Companion of the British Empire) in the Queen's Honours' List in 1977, he graciously declined it. He considered it inappropriate for a minister of the Gospel to be awarded such honours by the State.

He continued to chair the monthly Westminster Fellowship of ministers until 1980. When he queried whether, in the light of the rise in petrol prices, the men would prefer to meet bi-monthly, the response of one member from the Midlands ended all discussion: 'Even if it means hitch-hiking we will still come *monthly!*' Until the last couple of weeks of his life he received telephone calls from ministers needing advice and, though weak himself, he still brought blessing and encouragement to others.

His concern for a new generation of preachers, resulted in his being persuaded to chair a sponsoring committee of ministers from various church backgrounds, which led to the formation of the London

Above: Scene near Llanymawddwy

Facing page: Lloyd-Jones' last preaching engagement in Barcombe, Sussex, 1980

Theological Seminary (LTS). On 6 October 1977, people from all over Britain and overseas congregated for the opening meeting to hear Lloyd-Jones present the ways in which the training at the new institution would be different from what had prevailed over the last one hundred years. It was set up specifically to help train those called to be preachers and pastors and Lloyd-Jones chaired Seminary Board meetings, spoke at the opening services and occasionally addressed the students. Since his death, men from all parts of the world have been drawn to train at LTS often through first reading the sermons of Lloyd-Jones.

The Doctor's final evangelistic preaching tour was in May 1980 when he felt a little stronger. This would have been an exhausting schedule even for a more healthy younger person. It took him to the North of England, where Eddie Stobart, the founder of one of the country's most successful and prestigious road haulage firms, hastily arranged an inter-church meeting at the Methodist Central Hall, Carlisle, when over 700 people gathered at short notice. From there he journeyed to Glasgow to preach at the Jubilee celebrations of the Scottish Evangelistic Council. The following morning he was driven from Scotland to Wales where he preached on the Sunday evening to a handful of people in the tiny chapel at Llanymawddwy. From there he went to a mid-week meeting in Aberystwyth where 800 people, including over 300 students and young people, heard him preach for the last time. His condition was now deteriorating rapidly, and when most men would have given up the fight, he still kept a couple more appointments in the south of England before his final public appearance at the Westminster Fellowship on 7 July. To the end he had the interests of younger ministers in view and his closing prayer at the fraternal was most moving as he commended the men to the Lord.

Final days

As a preacher, Lloyd-Jones had been constantly directing people to Christ and to heaven. Now, as he faced the end of his own life in this world, what he had preached to others became even more precious to him. He died in his sleep in the early hours of Sunday morning, March 1, 1981, exactly thirteen years after his final service as minister of Westminster Chapel, and, appropriately for a Welshman, it was St David's Day. It was another form of cancer that eventually took his life. He had had his prostate gland removed in the autumn of 1976, but it became evident in the early spring of 1979 that the cancer had spread.

During the closing days of his life, when he had lost the strength to speak, he would communicate by a nod of the head, a gesture of the hand or write words on a scrap of paper. But his mind was alert to the end and quick to correct wrong conclusions. His consultant, a member of Westminster Chapel for many years, visited him less than a week before he died. When he suggested medication that would make him more comfortable, Lloyd-Jones shook his head. The consultant pressed him further, using the words of a hymn, that it grieved him to see his patient sitting there 'weary, worn and sad'. This was too much for Lloyd-Jones and with all the strength he could muster he whispered 'Not sad! Not sad!'

On the Thursday before his death he wrote with a shaky hand the following words in Welsh for his wife Bethan and the family, 'Do not pray for healing. Do not hold me back from the glory.'

Above: The river at Newcastle Emlyn. Summer holidays during the war years were spent visiting Martyn's relatives in the farms to the north

Burial and Thanksgiving

The funeral service was held in the little town of Newcastle Emlyn, dear to Lloyd-Jones from his boyhood days. On market day, Friday, 6 March, 1981, hundreds of people from all over Wales and beyond gathered to pay their last respects to this great man of God. The large, old, redundant Welsh Calvinistic Methodist chapel, where his wife's grandfather had ministered for many years, was re-opened for the occasion and was filled to capacity well before the coffin arrived.

The fifty-minute service began at two in the afternoon and was characterised, as one writer has put it, by its 'Welshness, assurance and triumph'. The service was conducted in English and the hymns were sung in Welsh. Bible verses describing Christ's victory over death and the resurrection hope were read and the sermon was based on Peter's words concerning the abundant entrance into Christ's everlasting kingdom that believers can enjoy (2 Peter 1:11).

After the service, the funeral cortège made its slow and solemn way to Gelli cemetery, a beautiful spot in the Cardiganshire hills not far out of town. Here the bodily remains of his wife's family lay buried including Ieuan Phillips, Bethan's brother and Martyn's best friend. During the short service at the graveside, over five hundred voices sang a verse of a Welsh hymn.

A month later, on 6 April a Thanksgiving Service was held at Westminster Chapel, London. It was an unforgettable experience.

Above: Newcastle Emlyn square

That great building was packed to overflowing, with some having to sit in the lesser halls. The singing was superb as nearly three thousand voices joined together in: *How good is the God we adore* and *Ten thousand times ten thousand*. It provided an unrepeatable reunion of people from all walks of life, young and old, family and friends, ministerial colleagues and former Westminster chapel members; from the Highlands and Islands of Scotland to Cornwall and the Channel Isles, from Europe and beyond. They had gathered to give God thanks for a man who had

Top: Bethel Presbyterian Church (Calvinistic Methodist) Newcastle Emlyn where the funeral service was held.
Right: Now used as a Chapel of Rest, it was built in 1869 as a place of worship on the site of an earlier, smaller building erected in 1820. Lloyd-Jones preached here during the first year of his ministry in Wales

Above: The burial in Gelli cemetery

Above: The congregation at Westminster Chapel for the Thanksgiving Service 6 April 1981

touched their lives for good in a variety of ways over a period of more than fifty years. There were tributes from the worlds of medicine, student work, literature, pastoral and pulpit ministry.

The obituary in *The Times* spoke of him as 'the last of a long line of great Welsh preachers', while the *Western Mail* described him as 'undoubtedly the finest pulpit orator of his generation and ... an outstanding leader of British Nonconformity.' Ten years later, a friend from the scholarly world, Professor FF Bruce of Manchester University, described him as 'a thoroughly humble man. Those who charged him with arrogance were wildly mistaken ... No one has arisen since to fill

the place which he occupied in the spiritual life of Britain.'

A simple black gravestone marks the spot where his body lies. The verse he had used to preach his first evening sermon in Sandfields, Port Talbot in November 1926 is quoted: 'For I determined not to know anything among you, save Jesus Christ, and him crucified.' (1 Corinthians 2:2)

His wife, Bethan, outlived him by ten years. She had given up a comfortable lifestyle in London to marry Martyn and to live in a terraced house in Aberavon. But she had no regrets and supported her husband in every way. Her own estimate of Lloyd-Jones is worth noting: 'No one will ever understand my husband unless

Above, left: The gravestone when first erected showing the low case 'i' (acceptable as a Welsh word), summarized a life that desired the 'I' to decrease that Jesus Christ might be preached and have all the glory

Above, right: The gravestone today

Above: Bethan Lloyd-Jones, July 1987

they first of all realise that he was a man of prayer and then an evangelist'. Bethan died in 1991 and her body now rests with his.

This great preacher of the 20th century still speaks through his printed sermons which have been translated into many languages including most European languages, Russian, Chinese and Korean. His voice can be heard on tape as some 1,600 recorded sermons of his have been made available to the public, and Premier Radio frequently broadcasts his messages. His preaching was gripping, fresh, full of good sense, and thoroughly biblical. He was never dry or predictable. Here was a genius who is still having a profound effect on many people's lives all over our world.

Carl Henry, the first editor of the influential American magazine

Christianity Today, interviewed Lloyd-Jones for the February 1980 edition. For many this was their first glimpse into the man himself and his background. When asked about future world history he was very pessimistic. He said, 'I think we are witnessing the breakdown of politics … Civilization is collapsing'. His parting words were: 'Flee from the wrath to come' and 'believe on the Lord Jesus Christ'.

Lloyd-Jones has been described as the last of the Welsh pulpit princes. It was significant that a century after his birth, an exhibition to commemorate his ministry was mounted at the National Library of Wales alongside an exhibition dedicated to Owain Glyndwr, the last of the Welsh Princes who fought for independence.

Above: Thomas Charles' body is buried beside the lake in St Beuno church graveyard, Llanycil

Below: Bethan Lloyd-Jones with the author's wife at the London Theological Seminary in 1986

BALA

LLANYCIL

A 494

1

2

3 4

5

6

TO DOLGELLAU

KEY TO BALA

1 FORMER CM THEOLOGICAL COLLEGE

2 BRYN-Y-GROES EVANGELICAL MOVEMENT

3 THOMAS CHARLES' HOUSE ON MAIN ST

4 THOMAS CHARLES' STATUE

5 LEISURE & INFORMATION CENT

6 TOMB OF THOMAS CHARLES IN LLANYCIL CEMETERY

BWLCH Y GROES (LOVELY VIEWS)

LLANYMAWDDWY

1

2

3

KEY TO LLANYMAWDDWY

1 BRYN UCHAF FARM

2 PARISH CHURCH

3 WELSH CONGREGATIONAL CHA

A 470

DINAS MAWDDWY

A 458

TRAVEL INFORMATION

Balsham, Cambs.

A pleasant little village south-east of Cambridge. There is a daily bus service from Cambridge bus station. By car from Cambridge, take A1307 crossing A11 to A604 to Linton then B1052; or from London take M11 to junction 9 then A11 to A604 and

B1052.

London Theological Seminary

104 Hendon Lane, Finchley, London N3 3SQ. ☎ 0208 346 7587. Junction 2 of the M1

onto A1/41 turn left at second set of lights into Hendon Lane (A504). It is also near the A406 (North Circular Road) where it meets the A1 and A41. Nearest underground is Finchley Central Northern Line (High Barnet and Mill Hill East branch). Bus routes 143,326 stop at the college, while routes 13, 82 and 260 stop nearby. Entrance to the college is in Wickliffe Avenue.

Bala

This small, largely Welsh speaking rural town is worth visiting with its large picturesque natural lake with sailing facilities. A light railway operates by the lakeside during the summer. Thomas Charles (1755–1814), an Anglican minister who became the second generation leader of the Calvinistic Methodists, ministered here most of his life and was instrumental with others in founding the British and Foreign Bible Society. He is associated with the story of Mary Jones and her Bible who did much to encourage him to obtain more Bibles in the Welsh language. He had a profound influence on Welsh religious, educational and cultural life.

Top: Newcastle Emlyn

Above: Plaque showing where Thomas Charles lived in Bala high street

Nearest railway station is Ruabon on the Shrewsbury to Wrexham line. Bus No, 94 between Wrexham and Barmouth runs via Ruabon and Bala. By car from Chester on A494 or A5 from Shrewsbury and Llangollen then A494.

Newcastle Emlyn

A small market town on the river Teifi. The castle originally built by the Welsh and repaired by Edward 1, was a royalist stronghold in the English civil war. Gelli cemetery is about a mile out of the town on the left hand side

NEWCASTLE EMLYN

TO CARDIGAN

A 484

RIVER TEIFI

TO LAMPETER

A 475

TO CARMARTHEN

A 484

KEY

1 GELLI CEMETERY

2 CATTLE MARKET

3 BETHEL CHAPEL

4 CASTLE

of the A484 to Cardigan. Bus Nos. 460,461 from Carmarthen to Cardigan stop here. By car from Carmarthen on A484.

Llanymawddwy

This hamlet can only be reached by car or walking. It lies on a narrow steep road between Llanuwchllyn on A494 and Dinas Mawddwy on A470. There are wonderful views from the top of the Bwlch, where there is a place to park. The nearest town is Bala. The Anglican church at Llanymawddwy was where Thomas Charles first ministered.

Right: *Statue of Thomas Charles outside the Welsh Presbyterian Chapel in Bala*

Above: Lloyd-Jones viewing the scenery from the Bwlch, near Llanymawddwy, in 1977

SELECT BIBLIOGRAPHY

Murray, Iain H. *D. Martyn Lloyd-Jones The First Forty Years 1899–1939*, Banner of Truth Trust, 1982. ISBN 0 85151 353 0 and *D. Martyn Lloyd-Jones The Fight of Faith 1939–1981*, Banner of Truth Trust, 1990, ISBN 0 85151 564 9. This two-volume work is the standard and detailed account of his life.
Catherwood, Christopher *Martyn Lloyd-Jones A Family Portrait*, Kingsway Publications, 1995. ISBN 0 86065 816 3
  This gives further glimpses into the human side of Lloyd-Jones.
Lloyd-Jones, Bethan *Memories of Sandfields 1927–1938*. Banner of Truth Trust, 1983.

ISBN 0 85151 366 2
  It includes accounts of some of the converts at Sandfields.
  Sermons and Addresses by Lloyd-Jones are published in the UK by Banner of Truth Trust, 3 Murrayfield Road, Edinburgh EH12 6EL; Bryntirion Press, Bryntirion, Bridgend, Wales CF31 4DX; Hodder & Stoughton Ltd, 338 Euston Road, London NW1 3BH; Kingsway Publications, Lottbridge Drive, Eastbourne, BN23 6NT.
  Tape recordings of his sermons can be obtained from: MLJ Recordings Trust, 2 Caxton House, Wellesley Road, Ashford, Kent TN24 8ET; Rev. I.M. Densham, 15 Ayr Terrace, St Ives, Cornwall TR26 1ED.

THE AUTHOR

Philip Eveson has degrees from the universities of Wales, Cambridge and London. He was ordained to the Calvinistic Methodist Christian ministry in 1968 and has pastored churches in South Wales and London. His grandfather and father first heard Lloyd-Jones preach in the 1930s and Philip heard him on numerous occasions as a boy in his home town of Wrexham, North Wales, as well as later in London. He was closely involved with Lloyd-Jones in the establishment of the London Theological Seminary where he has lectured for over twenty-five years and is now the Principal.

A SUMMARY OF MARTYN LLOYD-JONES' LIFE

20 December 1899	Born in Cardiff, South Wales
Spring 1905	Moved to Llangeitho, Cardiganshire (now Ceredigion)
January 1910	Escaped from house fire
1911	Won second place at Tregaron County School
August 1914	Moved to Westminster, London
January 1915	Entered St Marylebone Grammar school
1916	Entered St Bartholomew's Hospital Medical School
1918	Brother Harold, aged 20, died of Spanish influenza
1921	Gained his MRCS, LRCP, MBBS with distinction in medicine
	Began work with Sir Thomas Horder, the royal physician
1922	Father died
1923	Awarded MD and became Chief Clinical Assistant to Horder
	Teaching at Bart's, engaging in research and a Harley Street physician
1925	Gained his MRCP
1925–26	Struggled over his call to become a preacher
8 January 1927	Married Dr Bethan Phillips
3 February 1927	Inducted into the pastorate at Sandfields, Aberavon
26 October 1927	Ordained as a Calvinistic Methodist minister and the birth of his first daughter, Elizabeth
1932	First visit to North America
1937	His second daughter, Ann, was born
	Second visit to North America
1 May 1938	Resigned from Sandfields
	Became temporary assistant to Campbell Morgan, Westminster Chapel
April 1939	Accepted the call to be Associate Minister with Campbell Morgan
4 September 1939	Induction service cancelled due to the outbreak of war

1941	Ministers' Fraternal began at the Chapel
1943	Campbell Morgan retired as minister of the Chapel
1945	Addressed the formal opening of the Evangelical Library in London
1946	Visit to Sweden
1947	Third visit to America, chairing the first IFES Conference
1949	Addressed the first IVF Conference in Wales
1950	First 'Puritan Conference' at Westminster Chapel
1956	Fifth visit to America
1961	Preached at the 350th anniversary of the AV at the Albert Hall, London
18 October 1966	Controversial address at the Evangelical Alliance Assembly, Central Hall
November 1967	British Evangelical Council address on Luther
	Preached at the first anniversary of the Aberfan disaster
1 March 1968	Surgery for cancer
29 May 1968	Decision to retire announced to the Chapel deacons
1969	Last address at the IVF Conference Swanwick
	Last visit to North America, lecturing on 'Preaching'
1971	Last address to IFES
February 1977	Preached at Sandfields for 50th anniversary of the start of his ministry
October 1977	Inaugural address at the opening of the London Theological Seminary
1978	Last annual visit to the EMW Ministers' Conference at Bala
1980	Final meetings in Scotland, Wales and England
1 March 1981	Died at home in Ealing, London
6 March 1981	Funeral service and burial at Newcastle Emlyn
6 April 1981	Thanksgiving Service at Westminster Chapel

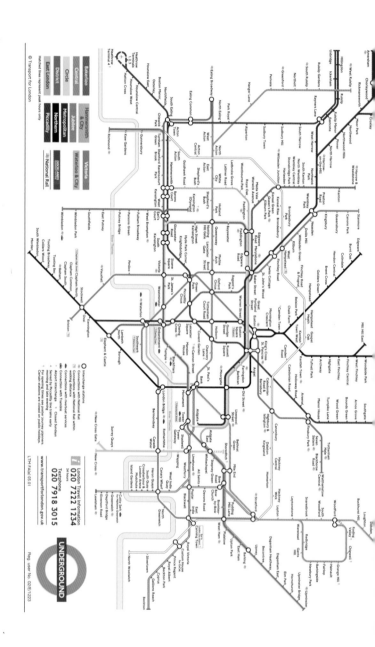